Beyond Playing Church

A Christ-Centered Environment for Church Renewal

Jesus Is Lord!

[signature]

Beyond Playing Church

A Christ-Centered Environment for Church Renewal

Dr. Michael Slaughter

Dedicated to

Carolyn, Kristen, and Jonathan

"gifts from God for the journey"

Acknowledgments

My deep appreciation goes to Cheryl Haerer who has worked diligently on this project, including the video series First Love, for almost five years. Her research, administrative and word processing skills, prayer, and friendship have made the completion of this book possible. My thanks to Elmo Flory for proof-reading the manuscript and his valuable suggestions.

I am indebted to Len Sweet and the people of United Seminary who have surrounded my life and encouraged the initial work. I will be forever grateful to the people of Ginghamsburg church, past and present, who have thrown gasoline on my burning bush along the way.

Contents

Foreword

by Howard Snyder

A Transformational Theology of Renewal

Fresh winds of renewal are blowing through many traditional churches in North America today. Even centuries-old "mainline" denominations like United Methodism (born out of a renewal movement!) are feeling fresh breezes sweep their elaborate corridors. Michael Slaughter's book is important evidence of these new winds.

As I talk with many people about renewal, I run into two general attitudes. Some say: traditional organized Christianity is dead. No hope. The only hope is to begin anew, to start over. Others say: Maybe God isn't through with the historic denominations. Maybe God is still in the business of resurrecting dry bones, opening streams in the desert, and granting pregnancy to overage bodies. Churches like Ginghamsburg United Methodist make me think this second view is closer to the truth.

This book is not primarily the story of Ginghamsburg church, however, but an applied theology of church renewal. Pastor Slaughter draws on the Ginghamsburg experience for examples, but also draws illustrations from church history. He wants to make it plain that genuine renewal isn't a matter of the right methods or techniques, but is spiritually and theologically grounded. This is a timely corrective to much literature on church growth and renewal which often turns sociology into theology: If it works, it must be God's will!

A common misconception is that church renewal and church growth are the same thing. They're not. This book is not *primarily* about church growth. Healthy, vital churches usually grow, but not always. Sometimes faithfulness brings decline in numbers, at least temporarily. John Wesley saw this. And many factors besides God's Spirit can produce growth. This book probes deeper than the question of growth to issues of vitality and spiritual authenticity.

In light of this, perhaps a word to readers who are members of small churches is in order. This is not a book, I think, about how you can have a megachurch. That's not the issue. It's a book about how to build lively, faithful churches. If broad-scale renewal comes to North American churches, it won't mean turning every little church into a big church. Rather, it will mean turning dead, or sleeping, or misdirected churches into vital outposts of the Kingdom of God. The world needs thousands of vital, world-transforming churches which are growing daily in discipleship and effective witness, regardless of their size. Ginghamsburg was an exciting, prophetic church when it numbered 100 or 200, as well as now that it is some ten times larger.

In his chapter on leadership, Pastor Slaughter quotes a newspaper reporter's comment about the Ginghamsburg church: This church "combines conservative evangelical theology with strong social activism." The reporter got it right. Here is a church that is evangelical without selling out to political ideology; activist without losing its focus on conversion and personal discipleship. This book lets the reader see the theological foundation underlying this biblical balance.

Beyond Playing Church is not the full story or the last word on church renewal, of course. No book

could be. Much more could be written on some
themes only touched on here. But this is an excellent
resource that can—and I hope will—spark fresh renewal in many churches across the land.

—Howard A. Snyder

Introduction

An Awakening Church?

It was Super Bowl Sunday. After preaching three morning services and grabbing a quick bite to eat, I reluctantly got into my car to drive a couple of hours across Ohio to speak at a Protestant church from a major denomination in a sleepy county seat town. As I traveled through rural Ohio that bright, crisp January afternoon, my mind was traveling also, looking at all the possibilities of the evening to come. Surely when this special Family Night event was planned five months earlier, the organizers had not realized that it would be in direct competition with the Super Bowl. They would be lucky to have 20 to 30 people present and probably no one under the age of 40. I had even dressed down for the occasion by slipping into a comfortable sweater and a pair of slacks before leaving home.

When I arrived at the church about a half hour early I was greeted by Marilyn and her husband, Dave, who were organizing this family event. They were very enthusiastic about the possibilities. Marilyn expressed concern about the potential conflict of interest with the football game, but felt Christ had a special purpose for the evening. They had creatively played up the theme of the Super Bowl and they planned to begin the evening with a "Super Bowl Chili Supper."

As the fellowship hall began to fill, several people gathered around a TV to watch pregame events while others chatted with lifelong friends. I was surprised

by the number of people who had turned out for the
supper and wondered how many of them would
leave immediately after eating to make it home in
time for the kickoff. A contemporary Christian group
sang several songs during the dinner and then several
of the youth from the church who had formed a
music group shared two original songs. The people
really seemed to be enjoying themselves!

When it came time for me to speak I noticed that
no one was leaving. Two new groups of people were
just arriving from other local churches and the hosts
began setting up extra chairs. I had expected the Super
Bowl to be a major detraction, but the fellowship hall
was filled with old and young alike who were eager
to experience the renewing power of Jesus Christ.

As I looked around the room I thought to myself,
"In this post-modern age, when 70 percent of women
under the age of 47 work outside the home, surely
these people had something else to do on Sunday
evening." People are just plain physically, mentally,
and spiritually exhausted, trying to keep up the pace
of raising children and paying bills in dual-income
and single-parent households. When we get home, we
want to stay there. The video market and home pizza
delivery industry flourish because of our baby boom-
er tendency to "cocoon" in the security of our homes.

I had expected distraction and sparse attendance.
Hunger, enthusiasm and personal expressions of new
purpose, discovered through a relationship with Jesus
Christ, are what I found. The people of God have
experienced enough games. On this Super Bowl evening they were demonstrating a deep inner longing to
make their lives count for a purpose greater than
themselves. The same transforming power of God
that I see working in the lives of my brothers and
sisters at Ginghamsburg I could see in the faces of
these people. They were longing for a deeper experience of God.

As I drove home that night I could not help but think about what was happening in my denomination. Many of our vital signs and statistics say we are a dying church with a graying membership and declining rolls. But wait—I see other signs! As I share the Ginghamsburg story I see enthusiasm and desire that can't be measured by statistics alone.

As I travel to churches across the country, I see evidence of renewed hunger for a living faith. I see people who are tired of playing church and are trying to find a way to *be* the church. Signs indicate people have a renewed interest in the Word and the world. I hear from people who are longing for a deeper experience of God's Spirit. New Sunday school classes and Bible study groups are starting. Unchurched people are visiting our churches with refreshing openness. Pastors are talking about ministry and not maintenance. Lay people are going on the offensive, organizing small-group fellowships and outreach ministries. Bishops are discussing vital congregations and the development of faithful disciples as the priority of the church. Stale mission statements are growing into challenging vision statements. There are islands of health and hope where the church seems to be focusing on relationships more than structure and organization. There is growing interest in the sacraments, and more and more of our people are boldly telling others about the transforming power of Jesus Christ in their lives.

Could it be . . . I thought to myself as I drove home through the clear winter night . . . that we are standing on the edge of a great spiritual awakening?

The Story of Ginghamsburg

My wife and I were returning to the office after a late lunch. As I turned into the parking lot of the patchwork campus of Ginghamsburg church I re-

marked to Carolyn, "This is truly a miracle. Look at
this place. It's an eyesore! With the corn field, unpaved
gravel parking lots, rusty garbage bins and mobile
trailers that we use for classrooms, it looks more like a
used-trailer lot than church grounds." More than once
we have had to corral the neighbors' cows in the
parking lot.

According to some church growth experts,
growth never should have occurred here. Our campus
has been located in the same non-highly visible loca-
tion since 1876. There are three small buildings and
four trailers. Most of our parking space is unpaved
farm field. Ginghamsburg is a small blip in the road
with approximately 20 houses. Tipp City, our mailing
address, has a population of 7,000 and is about four
miles away. Ginghamsburg is "urbanized country." By
most accounts this is definitely a non-church growth
environment. Yet in the last 14 years Ginghamsburg
had grown to be the largest United Methodist church
in Ohio in the areas of worship and Sunday school
attendance, size of staff and budget.

Ginghamsburg church has a history that is fairly
typical of many smaller mainline-denomination
churches across the country. It was founded in 1863;
the small red-brick and white-frame building where
we worshiped until 1984 was built in 1876. Through
the years the membership flitted between 80 and 120,
while the worship attendance ranged between 20 and
90 people. Most pastors stayed two to three years,
with the longest pastorate prior to my coming being
five years.

The average attendance in the fall of 1974 was
hovering around 20 people and the annual income of
the church was between $5,000 and $6,000. The people
were struggling to pay the utility bills and the student
pastor's salary. As the church was clearly in the grasp
of institutional death, the district superintendent
offered the people one last opportunity before the

doors of the church were to be permanently closed.
He sent Jim Worley, a middler student at United Theological Seminary, to Ginghamsburg.

Jim did two things: He began telling the people
about his personal experience with Jesus Christ, and
he taught about the church's need to be a covenant
community of radical love. Everything the church did
needed to be centered around a commitment to the
person of Jesus Christ, within the context of a loving,
supportive fellowship.

Under his leadership, the church began meeting
together every Thursday night for a potluck supper.
One Saturday night each month they met in different
homes. They called this meeting JOY (for Jesus, others, and you), and encouraged each other to bring
unchurched friends who could be supported by this
fellowship. Much like the church described in the
book of Acts, they not only held worship services in
their small two-room facility, "they broke bread at
home and ate their food with glad and generous
hearts . . . " (Acts 2:46).

By the time I was appointed to Ginghamsburg
United Methodist Church in April of 1979, the worship attendance had grown to 130 people on Sunday
morning with 95 in Sunday school and a membership
of 137. The annual budget was $27,000.

Thirteen years later our weekend worship attendance averages close to 1300 with over 800 in Sunday
school. More than 2,500 people would identify Ginghamsburg church as their church home but because
of our membership standard we have only 824 members. The annual budget is over $1,200,000 with an
additional $180,000 directed toward special mission
projects. We currently have 14 full-time and 16 part-
time staff people. Each week more than 30 families
visit Ginghamsburg church for the first time. The
church supports a resale clothing store, a women's
counseling center, a food pantry, a community crisis

ministry, a care and counseling center, three children's clubhouses in the inner city of Dayton and
Troy, Ohio, and a furniture warehouse in our local
area. All of us who have been experiencing this fresh
wind of the Spirit are continually awed by God's
work of grace.

We began this journey with some questions. Will
people get turned off by new worship forms? Would a
clear focus on Jesus as Lord and a tougher membership standard drive people away? We did lose about
30 of the original church members. The loss was
painful. Yet we heard the voice of Christ call us forward to risk the unknown. The people were willing
to risk doing a new thing.

The graph on the following page indicates worship attendance, Sunday school attendance and membership patterns since 1978.

At my denomination's governing conference in
Baltimore in 1984, delegates adopted the ambitious
goal of doubling our church's membership to 20
million by 1992. Not only did we not reach that goal
by 1992, but the church has continued to decline at
the rate of more than a thousand members a week.[1]
Needless to say, much attention has been given to
growing churches. The emphasis on church growth is
matched only by the flood of literature on the subject. Space needs, staffing, parking, promotion, calling
programs, and small-group ministry all get ample
attention. *But techniques must never be the focus of
growth!* The emphasis should never be on container
over content or task over spirit.

I have been given many opportunities during the
last few years to share Ginghamsburg's story in conference, district and local church meetings across our
denomination. Many times I have had the feeling that
people were expecting me to share a list of things to
do or programs to try so their churches could experience growth like that at Ginghamsburg church.

Ginghamsburg United Methodist Church Worship Attendance, Church Membership, and Sunday School Attendance, 1978-1992

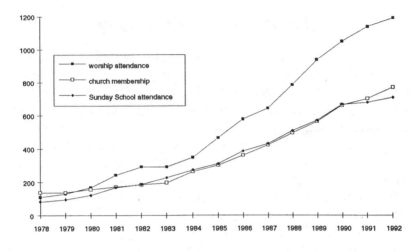

Figure 1

When I really began to look closely at what was happening at Ginghamsburg church, however, I could not link the main causes of growth with any specific techniques. In some cases we grew in spite of weak techniques. Growth seemed to be directly related to a work of the Spirit rather than our efforts alone. In some instances growth has meant allowing God to take us in directions we didn't really plan to go.

What I was able to identify, however, was a theology of renewal that prepared the people of Ginghamsburg church for the transforming work of God's Spirit. True renewal has more to do with theology than techniques. Techniques can be useful as tools to manage ministry but should never become the goal in themselves. Techniques need to have a solid theologi-

cal foundation. Techniques can be useful for getting
people into the church but they won't stay unless
they find spiritual authenticity. Advertising can gen-
erate customer traffic, but only the Spirit can transform human lives.

What is Renewal Theology?

Each great awakening throughout nearly 2,000
years of church history has employed different techniques. Altar calls, concerts of prayer, inquiry meetings, camp meetings, Wednesday night services, men's
breakfasts, small-group meetings, and a vast array of
liturgical forms have helped carry the gospel message
to diverse cultures. Church-growth techniques change
with cultures and historical time periods, but an
identifiable renewal theology is universal to every
revitalization throughout the history of the church.

In Ezekiel 37, the prophet is led by the Spirit of
God into a valley of dry bones, bones that represented
life from another time. A very significant question is
asked: "Can these bones live?" (Ezekiel 37:3) Can there
be life again where there is now death and decay? Is
total transformation possible? Can dry institutions be
transformed into vital movements?

> "Thus says the LORD God to these bones: I will
> cause breath to enter you, and you shall live. I
> will lay sinews on you, and will cause flesh to
> come upon you, and cover you with skin, and
> put breath in you, and you shall live...." I
> prophesied as he commanded me, and the
> breath came into them, and they lived, and
> stood on their feet, a vast multitude (Ezekiel
> 37:5-6, 10).

The prophetic message from God opens God's
people to the Spirit of revitalization. It is a transforming work of the Spirit that turns dry bones into the

living body of Christ and mobilizes a vast army of reformers. Renewal is God-breathed, not program planned!

The church in Ephesus could have been considered successful in many areas. They were a hard working church that believed in practicing what they preached. The people were known for their good deeds and sound doctrine. When the going got tough they did not quit. The Christians at Ephesus were committed to the work of the church in good times and bad, yet the church had one critical flaw. The people had forsaken their first love. They had gotten so busy doing the work of the Lord that they had forgotten the Lord of the work. The messenger of the Lord was calling them to repent and return to their first love (Revelation 2:1-7). The call was to remember first principles—the principles of renewal.

The church has been universally committed to six theological principles during every period of renewal:[2]

1. **The Lordship Principle:** a clear focus on Jesus Christ as the object of faith
2. **The Biblical Principle:** scriptural truth as the primary source for what we believe and do
3. **The Liturgical Principle:** discovery of new worship forms
4. **The Covenant Principle:** commitment to the integrity of membership
5. **The Priesthood Principle:** equipping the laity for ministry
6. **The Leadership Principle:** spiritual entrepreneurship

Commitment to the prophetic message of these theological principles is essential for renewal to take place in the church today.

A Definition of Church Renewal

Church renewal is more than an increase in numbers and budgets. Many gimmicks can be employed to get people to come and sit in church pews. If our only goal is to increase attendance, we could even pay people to attend church. But until people become committed to being faithful to the will of God, their attendance is no more meaningful than membership in any other human organization or club. Church renewal is people in community with each other, dreaming God's vision, believing Christ's victory, and living out the Spirit's work. The evidence of renewal will be seen in transformed lives.

Let me share with you a story of a family in our congregation that demonstrates the power of God's transforming presence.

A Mother's Story [3]

"Mom, being around Mike now is like, well, almost like having a new brother." As I looked at our youngest son, his words were a reminder to me of what God had done in Mike's life. Yes, Mike was a new man, a changed life, a testimony to God's grace. With Michael's permission I'd like to share his story, our story, with you.

I don't ever remember saying to God out loud or even in prayer that I expected our children to be problem-free or perfect. But somewhere in the deep recesses of my heart I guess I did believe the Lord would somehow put his stamp of approval on their lives. After all, as parents we were certainly doing all the right things. Bill and I became Christians when our oldest sons were two and four; a third son was born a year later. We worked at maintaining a Christian home, went to a Bible-believing church three times a week, and we even enrolled our three sons in a Christian school. Surely God would bless our efforts and our family.

But as I stood in the driveway of our home on that June night in 1984, I didn't feel very blessed by God. My heart was hurting like never before. I screamed at God in anger. What happened to the perfect plan? Where was God anyhow? Our oldest son had graduated that afternoon from high school, and in a few short hours had let us know he had no intentions of following his parents' Christian lifestyle or anything that resembled it.

That night would be the first of many nights as Bill and I watched Mike being sucked into all the garbage the world had to offer. He seemed so angry and unhappy as he plummeted from one bad experience to another. It was a very painful time for our whole family. A low point came when we had to ask Mike to move from our home, as we could no longer tolerate his choices for his life. This was a mutual decision, as Michael wasn't happy with our lifestyle, either.

As we watched our son leave our home that night we were filled with mixed feelings of grief and relief. It had been a long year. We still weren't sure we had made the right decision, but we had to think of our other two sons at home. Our pastor had told us there were rules and laws of a Christian home. Rules could be changed, but laws couldn't be broken, and Michael had certainly crossed the line. So we released our son to his choices, knowing it was a downward track for him. We had exhausted all of our human efforts as parents, and now we had to put feet on something we had given lip service to for the past 20 years—trusting God with our son. We knew in our hearts God knew far better than we the plan for Mike's life.

We didn't see much of Michael after that. Occasionally he would come by for Sunday dinner, always looking worse than the time before. It was evident things were falling apart in his life. We continued to watch and pray.

During this time the Lord began to work in our lives as parents. He taught us in a mighty way the power of prayer. He impressed on us to share our burden for Mike with as many praying people as possible. Consequently, Mike was on prayer lists all over the country from Texas to Wisconsin to California. In our own church, this body held us up as a family in prayer. I vividly remember an Ash Wednesday service where we were to place prayer requests on the altar and others would come and pray for that request. We joined a growth group that many times carried us through the roughest times in prayer.

It was also during this time the Lord began to reveal to us, in a loving way by his Spirit, the faultiness of some of our parenting. This was a painful time because our hearts meant well, but our doctrine had been harsh, thus creating a home full of legalistic do's and don'ts. We recognized ourselves as having similar problems as the pharisees. We had to go before the Father with a repentant heart and ask him to cover our blunders with our children.

He also taught us about offering unconditional love, avoiding unrealistic expectations and providing acceptance and forgiveness. All of this we had received from the Father, but we had failed to parent our children and especially our first-born son this way. Those were months of healing as we received from our Lord his shower of grace. We continued to pray for Mike.

One afternoon in early May Mike came through the back door of our home and sat down at the bar in the kitchen. We talked for a few minutes. He looked tired, even old for his twenty years. It was obvious life was beating away at him. "Mom," he began, "I need you to pray for me."

"We've been praying, son," I replied. Mike began to cry. The story was sad, all the things that can happen in a life running from God. He was broken in spirit. The tears were the first since he was about 10 years old; a long time coming. We did pray that day for God to work in Mike's life for the good. Sometimes it's hard to know what to ask God for in specifics. This was one of those times.

Mike left that day and we were encouraged; No, we were thankful. God was moving. We began to see him more after that. He would drop by for dinner or just to visit. The problems were still there, but his heart was beginning to change and so were ours. He asked if he could move back into our home. We weren't sure. We were scared, but eventually we worked out sort of a verbal contract with our son, and Michael came home.

It would be a long road back. Healing needed to take place, and that would take time. It would be a lot of work, long talks, apologies, tears, laughter, and continued trusting in God.

Our prayers changed for Michael at that point. He no longer needed our constant prayers for protection; he needed to walk his own walk with the Father. Most of all he needed to know God's love, acceptance and forgiveness. So that's how we prayed. It was a wonderful time to trust God once again.

Mike struggled with many issues during that healing time. He had been drained of his self esteem and motivation. He needed to recognize his potential and value as God's man. He began attending church again and found love and support here at Ginghamsburg church. But most of all he found the Father who had been waiting all the time.

Finally, the time came when Mike became interested in his future. He began to look at various colleges and chose Taylor University, entering

as a freshman in the fall of 1988. He took with him
his life verse, Jeremiah 29:11 (NIV),

> *"For I know the plans I have for you," declares*
> *the Lord, "plans to prosper you and not to harm*
> *you, plans to give you hope and a future."*

Becoming a student took some adjustment
for Mike. Concentration came hard and being
older than most freshmen he felt uncomfortable.
He was given the opportunity to be a hall advisor
in his dorm, and Mike discovered he had many
gifts in dealing with people. He was respected and
admired by his peers. It was a blessing to watch
Mike during that time develop into who God was
making him.

In May of 1992, Michael graduated from
Taylor with a double major in psychology and
business. The graduation was wonderful, and as
the class marched across the field, we quickly
found our son in the crowd. Jeremiah 29:11 was
taped on the top of his graduation cap. We cried
happy, thankful tears.

Michael is now working as a county proba-
tion officer. He is looking at several grad programs for the near future. He is living at home for
the time being, and we are enjoying the years the
locusts had eaten as God restores our relationship.

We share Michael's story for several reasons.
First, to encourage you that are struggling to
know God cares and answers prayer. He still
performs miracles. Claim his plan for you as
Jeremiah 29 promises. Secondly, to give glory and
honor to Jesus Christ, the only One who gives new
life.

Social Impact

Renewal is personal but also spills out on social
institutions as well. Every great awakening has had a
resulting major effect on the moral, economic, politi-

cal and cultural foundations of society itself. Historian William G. McLoughlin goes so far as to say that the great awakenings in American history have influenced most of our nation's social reforms. He contends that they are "the catalysts of social change."[4]

As the church becomes spiritually renewed it moves against evil forces that oppress people. It was a renewed church with a transformed people that fought slavery and illiteracy and sent armies of missionaries around the world to teach, preach and heal. Wesleyan renewal brought a moral-spiritual strength that averted a potential civil war in England and created many just changes in a corrupt neo-industrial age. The church was at the heart of the struggle against racism in the 1960s, and a renewed church is needed today to carry on the continuing battle against the demonic forces of apartheid in South Africa and the growing tide of racism that is raising its ugly head again in the United States.

A ministry that is holistic, that sees people as physical and spiritual beings with both physical and spiritual needs, must be happening if it is truly a renewal of the Spirit of God. Transformation will occur in the lives of the people. The justice of God will be seen in the community of the transformed. As the result of the revival on the day of Pentecost the believers sold their possessions and shared with anyone as they had need (Acts 2:45). This spirit of love can be manifested only by a work of the Spirit of God—not by gimmicks and human enthusiasm.

Numerical growth is also important in the renewal of the life of the church.

> So those who welcomed his message were baptized, and that day about three thousand persons were added (Acts 2:41).

> And day by day the Lord added to their number those who were being saved (Acts 2:47).

But many of those who heard the word believed; and they numbered about five thousand (Acts 4:4).

Yet more than ever believers were added to the Lord, great numbers of both men and women (Acts 5:14).

Numbers are important because each number represents an individual life. When individuals realize the infinite worth they have in the eyes of God and are transformed through faith in Jesus Christ, they become willingly committed to being part of God's awakening in the church and the world.

This book is an attempt to remind the church of first principles—a call to return to the First Love.

Notes

1 Richard B. Wilke, *And Are We Yet Alive?* (Nashville: Abingdon Press, 1986), 26.

2 Major periods of growth and renewal: New Testament church and its rapid missionary expansion before it was legalized under Constantine, 313 A.D.; The conversion of St. Augustine and his influence over the church, Fourth Century; The Reformation and Counter-Reformation in the Catholic Church, 1517-1648; The Wesleyan Renewal, 18th century; and the two Great Awakenings in American history, under Jonathan Edwards, 18th century and under Charles Finney, 19th century. The current renewal is seen throughout various pockets of the church and expressed in various forms like the charismatic movement and the rapid growth of the church in third-world countries.

3 Story used with permission of Bill and Norma Stout, faithful servants in Christ's mission at Ginghamsburg United Methodist Church

4 William G. McLoughlin, "Revivalism," in *The Rise of Adventism,* ed. Edwin Scott Gaustad (New York: Harper and Row, 1974), 132.

The Lordship PRINCIPLE

*A Clear Focus on
Jesus Christ
as the Object of Faith*

Chapter One

For several mainline Protestant denominations this broadening of the belief system has reached the point that "inclusive" or "pluralistic" has replaced that original doctrinal statement as a rallying cry. Thus the original reason for the existence of that denomination has been eroded . . .

The most difficult charge before the mainline Protestant denomination seeking to carve out a long-term and more productive future will be to define and project an identifiable theological position.[1]

Lyle E. Schaller

The Object of Faith

The first and most important theological element that I was able to identify in the growth of Ginghamsburg church was the clear focus on the person, work, and authority of Jesus Christ. He is the reason behind every action we take. "For 'In him we live and move and have our being' " (Acts 17:28).

The earliest Christian creed was simply "Jesus is Lord!" This early Jewish sect was considered rigid and unbending in their absorption with Jesus Christ and their insistence on his uniqueness in God's plan of salvation. From Matthew to Revelation we find a clear witness to Jesus' identity as God's unique son and his absolute authority as the governing Lord of the universe. For example:

> "Therefore let the entire house of Israel know with certainty that God has made him both Lord and Messiah, this Jesus whom you crucified" (Acts 2:36).

> "There is salvation in no one else, for there is no other name under heaven given among mortals by which we must be saved" (Acts 4:12).

The author of the Gospel of John confirms the witness of the early Christian community concerning the uniqueness of Jesus:

> "I am the way, and the truth, and the life. No one comes to the Father except through me" (John 14:6).

> "Whoever has seen me has seen the Father. How can you say, 'Show us the Father'? Do you not believe that I am in the Father and the Father is in me?" (John 14:9-10).

> "I am the resurrection and the life. Those who believe in me, even though they die, will live, and everyone who lives and believes in me will never die. Do you believe this?" (John 11:25).

For the New Testament church Jesus was clearly more than a good moral teacher who pointed to God. He was the object of faith.

A Vague Theism

The church has a tendency to lose this clear focus on the person of Jesus Christ and to retreat into a vague theism. This can be seen in much of the theology of the 1960s: "God is love . . . love is God." For many of us

Jesus was just a guy holding sheep in a stained-glass window.

The message and focus of the New Testament church was not a vague concept of a benevolent God. It was a message of radical faith in the person of Jesus Christ. Again and again we read, "they preached Jesus and the resurrection." From the first chapter of Acts to the last, you find a clear, focused witness of salvation in Jesus Christ authenticated by the Resurrection.

This point cannot be overemphasized. Jesus was not the example. He was the cause of truth. Every act of the New Testament church was attributed to Jesus. Peter, in explaining the healing of a beggar who could not walk, proclaimed,

> "... let it be known to all of you, and to all the people of Israel, that this man is standing before you in good health by the name of Jesus Christ of Nazareth, whom you crucified, whom God raised from the dead. This Jesus is 'the stone that was rejected by you, the builders; it has become the cornerstone'" (Acts 4: 10-11).

The Jewish authorities considered this teaching about Jesus blasphemy against God. They were

> ... much annoyed because they were teaching the people and proclaiming that in Jesus there is the resurrection of the dead (Acts 4:2).

> So they called them and ordered them not to speak or teach at all in the name of Jesus (Acts 4:18).

It is important to understand this total preoccupation with the person of Jesus of Nazareth. For the primitive church, there was no identity in God or salvation apart from him.

> Everyone who believes that Jesus is the Christ has been born of God, and everyone who loves the parent loves the child (1 John 5:1).

Who is it that conquers the world but the one who believes that Jesus is the Son of God? (1 John 5:5)

Those who believe in the Son of God have the testimony in their hearts. Those who do not believe in God have made him a liar by not believing in the testimony that God has given concerning his Son. And this is the testimony: God gave us eternal life, and this life is in his Son. Whoever has the Son has life; whoever does not have the Son of God does not have life (1 John 5: 10-12).

Why did the New Testament church make such bold, sweeping assertions? These people were thoroughly convinced that this carpenter from Nazareth had literally been resurrected from the grave. God had confirmed the uniqueness of Jesus by this great historical event. To the believers in the early church the Resurrection was not a symbolic faith statement but a supernatural intervention of God in space and time. Paul confirms this literal interpretation.

... Christ died for our sins in accordance with the scriptures, and that he was buried, and that he was raised on the third day in accordance with the scriptures, and that he appeared to Cephas, then to the twelve. Then he appeared to more than five hundred brothers and sisters at one time, most of whom are still alive, though some have died. Then he appeared to James, then to all the apostles. Last of all, as to one untimely born, he appeared also to me (1 Corinthians 15: 3-8).

Paul is listing eyewitnesses. He is documenting and validating the accuracy of this event. That is why he places such an emphasis on the appearance to five hundred witnesses "at one time" and emphasizes that

"most are still alive." Paul is saying, "If you don't believe me, go and check it out for yourselves with
many others who witnessed this great event." He goes
on to say,

> . . . and if Christ has not been raised, then our
> proclamation has been in vain and your faith
> has been in vain. . . . If Christ has not been
> raised, your faith is futile and you are still in
> your sins. Then those also who have died in
> Christ have perished. If for this life only we
> have hoped in Christ, we are of all people
> most to be pitied (1 Corinthians 15: 14, 17-19).

Paul is boldly asserting, "If the body of Jesus is lying
lifeless and molding in some grave, then our faith is
worthless. He is not who he said he was, and we are
the greatest fools of all. So let's all go home and quit
playing church. Let's quit lying to people by telling
them that God did something that he really didn't do."

It is very important to recognize Paul's concern
for the credibility of his unwavering acceptance of
the Resurrection and the integrity of his testimony. In
1 Corinthians 15:15 Paul gives a clear statement to the
intent of total honesty in his witness when he says, in
effect, "If we said Christ rose from the grave, and he
didn't, not only would we be liars, but we would be
lying against God because we said that God has done
something that God has not done."

The New Testament church believed in a literal,
not symbolic, Resurrection. For this reason they had a
clear conviction that Jesus Christ was different from
any other person who ever lived. No one had ever said
or done the things that Jesus did. The early Christians
were so convinced of the validity of the witness
concerning Jesus and the fact of the Resurrection that
they were willing to lay down their lives for this man.
These people were willing to forsake everything that
they knew. They were shunned, persecuted, consid-

ered a cult, thrown out of the temple, and impris-
oned—not for a vague theism, but because they believed that Jesus Christ was the living Lord, the object
of their faith.

Renewal—Returning to the First Love

"I know your works, your toil and your patient
endurance. I know that you cannot tolerate
evildoers; you have tested those who claim to
be apostles but are not, and have found them
to be false. I also know that you are enduring
patiently and bearing up for the sake of my
name, and that you have not grown weary. But
I have this against you, that you have aban-
doned the love you had at first. Remember
then from what you have fallen; repent, and
do the works you did at first" (Revelation 2: 2-
5).

The church's first major struggle after the early
persecutions was the rise of great heresies. They were
considered heresies because of their interpretation of
the most fundamental Christian doctrine—the person
of Christ.

Arianism, one of the most widely held of these
heresies, was rejected at the Council of Nicaea in 325
and again at the Council at Constantinople in 381
because it blatantly denied the full diety of Christ.
The growing popularity of the heresies forced the
church to develop a formal body of teaching on the
person and work of Christ. One of the early writers of
this theology, who insisted on the deity of Jesus, was
Saint Augustine of Hippo (354-430). He is considered
to be one of the greatest theologians in the early
church. The Protestant and Catholic reformers were
greatly influenced by his work more than a thousand
years later.

Augustine had a dramatic conversion experience at the age of 33 after years of philosophical search and sensual living. He had struggled with the power of sin and the weakness of the human will and could identify with Paul's statement, "For I do not do the good I want, but the evil I do not want is what I do" (Romans 7:19).[2] After his conversion he saw Christ as more than a mere man or moral teacher, but "that He merited the highest authority."[3] He believed that conversion necessitated putting "on the Lord Jesus Christ."[4]

Augustine clarified a biblical theology for the church that stressed human impotence without divine grace, justification by faith in Christ as opposed to works, and Christ's sacrifice as being all-sufficient and the only sufficient sacrifice for salvation.[5] Augustine's clear Christ-centeredness spurred the renewal that occurred during both the Protestant Reformation and the Counter-Reformation in the Catholic Church during the sixteenth and seventeenth centuries.

Martin Luther, a priest and former Augustinian monk, objected to the medieval-church system and its departure from Paul's biblical teaching, which affirmed that salvation is found simply through faith in Jesus Christ and Jesus Christ alone. Luther emphasized that justification was not obtained by performing good works. He felt that the focus and authority of the church had shifted from the person of Christ to the institution. Luther equated this realization to a Damascus-road experience.[6] Through his teachings the church began to experience transformational renewal by rediscovering the First Love.

Renewal happens as the church moves from a vague theism to a clear faith in Jesus Christ. The focus of the church is not church, but Jesus! God is made known to us in Christ. Faith comes alive in Christ. Lives are transformed and empowered through Christ.

The same movement of the Spirit that affected the reformers was also moving among those who

were committed to staying in the Catholic Church. A
clear focus on Christ as the focus of faith and worship
was also at the heart of the Counter-Reformation. A.
G. Dickens writes,

> And even after Luther's revolt, the highest
> Catholic achievements were those of men and
> women who believed themselves to be seek-
> ing Christ rather than fighting Luther.[7]

Ignatius Loyola (1491-1556) was to the Catholic
Church and the Counter-Reformation what Luther
was to the Protestant Reformation. Loyola had a conversion experience six years after Luther, but was
committed to renewal within the Catholic Church. He
founded the Society of Jesus (the Jesuits) with the
express purpose of renewing the church and taking
Christ to the unchurched people of the world. The
Jesuits shared Christ with a missionary zeal. Dickens
states:

> To their leadership Ignatius brought far more
> than a series of heroic gestures: the new soci-
> ety grouped itself not only round the man but
> round a scheme of devotion clearly embodied
> in his "Spiritual Exercises" ... the devotional
> method and idiom remained intensely Christ-
> ocentric.[8]

Ignatius Loyola was calling people back to following Christ in a radical way. The Jesuits and their focus
on Christ became the primary vehicle both for carrying renewal throughout the church and for reaching
the unchurched.

Teresa of Avila (1515-1582), from whom Mother
Teresa of Calcutta has taken her name, and St. John of
the Cross (1542-1591) were reformers who also played
key roles in the renewal movement within the Catholic Church. Both had a consuming passion to experience Christ and make him known. They taught the

church much about the necessity of personal time spent with Christ in prayer and meditation.

These reformers clearly understood that apart from a personal, dynamic growing relationship with Christ the church has no life. Christ is our life!

> I pray that out of his glorious riches he may strengthen you with power through his Spirit in your inner being, so that Christ may dwell in your hearts through faith. And I pray that you, being rooted and established in love, may have power, together with all the saints, to grasp how wide and long and high and deep is the love of Christ, and to know this love that surpasses knowledge—that you may be filled to the measure of all the fullness of God (Ephesians 3: 16-19, NIV).

John Wesley (1703-1791) grew up and began ministering in the Anglican Church of England, a church that had again cooled in its passion for Jesus Christ. His ministry was marked by years of frustration and uncertainty before his conversion on May 24, 1738. He had even confessed to the Moravian leader Peter Bohler that he doubted his own salvation. Shortly after a disastrous missionary journey to Georgia, Wesley wrote concerning his ignorance about Christ as the object of faith:

> In my return to England, January 1738, being in imminent danger of death, and very uneasy on that account, I was strongly convinced that the cause of that uneasiness was unbelief; and that the gaining a true, living faith was the 'one thing needful' for me. But still I fixed not this faith on its right object: I meant only faith in God, not faith in or through Christ. Again, I knew not that I was wholly void of this faith; but only thought I had not enough of it. So that when Peter Bohler, whom God prepared

for me as soon as I came to London, affirmed of true faith in Christ (which is but one) that it had those two fruits inseparably attending it, 'dominion over sin and constant peace from a sense of forgiveness,' I was quite amazed, and looked upon it as a new gospel. If this was so, it was clear I had not faith. . . . And accordingly the next day he came again with three others, all of whom testified, of their own personal experience, that a true living faith in Christ is inseparable from a sense of pardon for all past and freedom from all present sins.[9]

In the week that followed Wesley shifted his focus from a vague benevolent God to the living Christ.

In the evening I went very unwillingly to a society in Aldersgate Street, where one was reading Luther's preface to the Epistle to the Romans. About a quarter before nine, while he was describing the change which God works in the heart through faith in Christ, I felt my heart strangely warmed. I felt I did trust in Christ, Christ alone for salvation; and an assurance was given me that He had taken away my sins, even mine, and saved me from the law of sin and death.[10]

Wesley wrote this journal entry the following day.

The moment I awaked, "Jesus, Master," was in my heart and in my mouth; and I found all my strength lay in keeping my eye fixed upon Him, and my soul waiting on Him continually.[11]

Wesley was quickly branded an enthusiast by the church for his zealous insistence on conversion through personal faith in Jesus Christ. Pulpit after pulpit was closed to Wesley because he called the people to repent of their dead institutionalism and return to their first love in Jesus Christ. John Wesley rigidly believed and taught that there is no salvation apart from the atoning work of Jesus Christ. According to Burtner and Chiles, Wesley

> declares that turning from the atonement is equivalent to embracing deism or paganism; he regards either defection as disastrous to the life of faith.... A letter to William Law on this subject shows Wesley to have been accusing, even bitter, because he failed to find in Law's writings the gospel pronouncement of Christ's atoning work for man. Faith in this atoning work is for Wesley the sole way to salvation.[12]

The church has once again lost its clear focus on the person of Jesus Christ and his unique exclusive role in God's redemptive plan. But a new wind is blowing. New voices are being heard in the church.

These voices are reminding us that "in Christ God was reconciling the world to himself" (2 Corinthians 5:19). In Christ!

I want to add a word of caution. Renewal is much more than adding a little more Jesus to the mix. A little more Jesus won't work. Jesus has to be the absolute focus. It must be an all-or-nothing proposition. A clear focus on Jesus Christ as the object of faith and the cause of truth is the key for renewal. Clarity of focus is now more necessary than ever in a post-Christian age.

Absolute Authority

When persons enter into the covenant of membership with a local church in my denomination they are asked a crucial question: Do you confess Jesus Christ as your Lord and Savior and pledge your allegiance to his kingdom?

My family and I had the privilege of traveling and preaching in Germany during the summer of 1990. We were invited by a group of informal churches called *Gemeindes* that were born out of the Jesus movement during the 1960s and 1970s. These informal churches meet in rented buildings, beer gardens, YMCAs, and traditional church facilities during untraditional times. While the state church (Lutheran) has an older, more rural population, the membership of the *Gemeindes* is very young, almost exclusively under forty. Most are twenty-something.

While the *Gemeindes* are "unofficial," they offer an exciting approach to reaching unchurched people in a mainly unchurched culture. The *Gemeindes* tend to average between 30 and 200 in their meetings. Many are young university students. A great number are being drawn from the punk culture and even some of the "skin heads" are being transformed. Needless to say these informal congregations make for an interesting mix.

We had been in Germany for about two weeks. I was speaking on a Sunday evening to the congregation of *Rhema Gemeinde.* They were using the facilities of a Lutheran church in Darmstadt. The German language does not have a word for "Lord." To translate the word "Lord" the German people use the word "Herr." Herr means mister.

I was openly sharing my frustration in having to refer to Jesus as "Mister Jesus" instead of "Lord Jesus" and how the word was totally inadequate in expressing Jesus' true identity. A young man who was a master's student in engineering at a local university stood up in the back of the church and stated right in the middle of my discourse: "We may not have a word for Lord, but you Americans might as well not have. You don't know what it means."

He was right. His response was prophetic. Many of us in the Western church today have lost sight of what the word "Lord" means. For many it is just a title like "reverend" or "doctor" or "sir." So when we say "Lord Jesus" we really mean no more than "Mr. Jesus."

In the New Testament church, the meaning was clear. "Lord" meant the one who had absolute authority. Caesar was the only one who could be called "Lord" with a capital "L." The typical greeting on the street in the Roman empire would include the affirmation "Caesar is Lord." And the response would echo this affirmation of absolute authority, "Yes, Caesar is truly Lord." It was the law. To fail to publicly acknowledge Caesar's claim to deity and absolute authority could mean arrest and ultimately death.

The word also means "owner." A slave referred to his or her owner as "lord" with a small "l." This meant that the slave was bound to the authority of the master and lived totally in service to the master's will. The slave had no rights of his or her own. A slave's only possible response was complete obedience.

Many Americans have difficulty with the concept of obedience. We are used to a democracy that gives us many different choices and opportunities for input and involvement. We can choose where to live, what to do for a vocation, whom to marry, and the organizations we will join. We even choose what we want to believe or not believe. We can be Republican, Democrat, socialist or even Communist. At the heart of a democracy lies the concept of freedom of choice. Jesus, however, did not come proclaiming a democracy. He came proclaiming a kingdom.

There is a major difference between a kingdom and a democracy. In a democracy the people determine the rules of the game. They set up a charter or a constitution and participate in the running of the club or organization. Each person accepts a responsibility and there are dues and money-making projects to support the purpose. Each person has a vote or say in how the organization operates.

In a kingdom all rules are determined by the king. Each person is given a responsibility. A king does not have dues or money-making projects—he sets tariffs. He does not have to ask me for my consent—he commands! The biggest difference between a democracy and a kingdom lies in the concept of choice. In a democracy choice lies in the hands of the governed. In a kingdom choice lies solely with the king.

Many people in the church today treat the church like a democracy; the same rules that apply to the Girl Scouts and the Kiwanis apply to the church. It is often difficult to tell the difference between the church and many service clubs. We like to think of ourselves as "volunteers" who pick and choose what we will do for God and God's church. We even minimize the importance of the work when we go through the annual nomination process by asking people to "help out" in non-costly ways:

> "You wouldn't want to help us out by serving on the education committee this year, would you?"

> "Well, I don't know. What's involved?"

> "Oh, not much, not much at all—you have to attend only one meeting a month."

At Ginghamsburg church we are realizing that it costs everything to follow Jesus. If we ask someone to carry out the trash and he or she asks what's involved, we now respond by saying "everything!"

The early church understood clearly the meaning of the affirmation "Jesus is Lord!" When Christians were greeted on the street with "Caesar is Lord" their response often caused much controversy. They recognized only one absolute authority and owner. "Jesus is Lord!" The Roman Colosseum did a tremendous business because of the Christians' stubborn insistence concerning Jesus' absolute authority.

Volunteer or Slave?

"Who among you would say to your slave who has just come in from plowing or tending sheep in the field, 'Come here at once and take your place at the table'? Would you not rather say to him, 'Prepare supper for me, put on your apron and serve me while I eat and drink; later you may eat and drink'? Do you thank the slave for doing what was commanded? So you also, when you have done all that you were ordered to do, say, 'We are worthless slaves; we have done only what we ought to have done!'" (Luke 17: 7-10).

Jesus quickly gets to the heart of the issue of the "volunteer" mentality of service in this passage. The word for "servant" is "bondslave." A bondslave or servant did not work for wages but lived under the authority and ownership of a master. The servant's ear was pierced and an earring with the emblem of the family of ownership was placed in that slave's ear. The earring meant that the slave was bound to that household for life.

Slaves had no rights or privileges. Individual identity was exchanged for the identity of the master. The initials on the earring became their own. Slaves did not have anything that was personal. Everything belonged to the master, even the clothes they had on their back. There was no distinction between work time and personal time for slaves. Every moment belonged to the master. That is the key point that Jesus is making in this parable.

Slaves in middle eastern culture rarely lived to see the age of 30. They were expected to be in the fields from first light to last light, six in the morning until about nine at night. On the way to and from the fields they had to milk and feed the livestock. When a slave came in after a grueling schedule the master did not say, "Oh, you poor slave. You have been working so hard all day. Why don't you take a quick shower and then come on over here and sit down in my recliner and I will get you the newspaper and a cool drink." Instead the master would say, "Slave, look at you—you are a mess. Hurry and get cleaned up and come back and get our drink orders and fix our supper."

Dinner in this culture was the highlight of the day. Without television or any of the other distractions that invade our family time, people actually stayed around the family table and talked to each other for most of the evening. They would lie prone around the table on pillows.

The supper meal was one of the most intimate parts of the day. It is the word Jesus uses when he says, "Listen! I am standing at the door, knocking; if you hear my voice and open the door, I will come in to you and eat with you, and you with me" (Revelation 3:20). The word translated "eat" in this passage literally means "supper meal," the intimate meal that was the highlight of the day.

Needless to say much preparation went into this meal. But guess who was responsible for preparing it? You guessed it—the good old bondservant. After a full day in the field and tending the animals the slave had to come in, clean up, and prepare a major dinner. Often this would also involve the oversight of entertainment. Only after the drinks were served, the food was on the table, the belly dancers were finished, and the master put to bed, could the slaves finally help themselves to any of the leftover food before falling exhausted into bed.

Jesus said that we must identify with that slave if we are to truly be his followers. We must come to that point of realizing, "we are unworthy servants; we have only done our duty." Volunteer is the language of the club. Slave is the language of the kingdom of God.

God's Choice—Not Mine

As the people of Jesus, we need to come to that place where we understand that the call of God always comes in the form of a command. Nowhere in Scripture do we hear God asking whether anyone would like to "help out."

In the third chapter of Exodus we find Moses working in his father-in-law's business. While on a business trip he has a personal encounter with God in which God calls him to go to Egypt and appear before Pharaoh. He is to tell Pharaoh that God has not been blind to the whole issue of oppression and segregation and that God expects Pharaoh to right the wrong by letting the Israelites go.

Moses, at this point, does not understand that the call of God upon his life is not a multiple-choice option. He proceeds to list reasons why it would be better for God to choose someone else: "Lord I can't do that.... I've never been to seminary.... I ... I'm not a very eloquent speaker. ... I even stutter. Pharaoh would never believe me ... I don't have any credentials.... Have you considered my brother Aaron? He is more polished than I ... Please send someone else ... anyone else!" Moses spends almost two chapters trying to talk his way out of the inevitable. Finally, after God has patiently listened to Moses' excuses, he reminds Moses that obedience is not an option.

A king does not ask for consent—he decrees. Jesus reminded his followers of this great truth when he said, "You did not choose me but I chose you. And I appointed you to go and bear fruit, fruit that will last" (John 15:16). We do not vote for Jesus or even choose Jesus. He is the absolute authority—the owner—the one who calls us and sends us. Our only response can be one of obedience. When we recognize the authority of Jesus Christ we realize that the ordering of our daily activities is God's choice—not ours.

Good Excuses

As they were going along the road, someone said to him, "I will follow you wherever you go." And Jesus said to him, "Foxes have holes, and birds of the air have nests; but the Son of Man has nowhere to lay his head." To another he said, "Follow me." But he said, "Lord, first let me go and bury my father." But Jesus said to him, "Let the dead bury their own dead; but as for you, go and proclaim the kingdom of God." Another said, "I will follow you, Lord; but let me first say farewell to those at my home." Jesus said to him, "No one who puts a hand to the plow and looks back is fit for the kingdom of God" (Luke 9:57-62).

A friend of mine had the opportunity to meet Mother Teresa while he was traveling in India. On a whim he decided to visit the Missionaries of Charity headquarters while he was staying in Calcutta. He wasn't even sure that Mother Teresa was in the country, but it was worth the chance.

After an adventurous cab trip through crowded streets Rob arrived at the simple structure that houses one of the greatest testimonies to the reality of the Resurrection in the world. Rob knocked at the door and a young novice in the simple white and blue sari of the Missionaries of Charity answered. Rob explained the intent of his mission. By the good graces of God, Mother Teresa was in the country. And even better, she was working in the headquarters this day.

The young disciple ushered my friend into a simple parlor. After a brief wait Rob could hardly believe his eyes. There she stood! A little frail, bent-over woman that overflowed with the presence of Jesus. She graciously spent 15 to 20 minutes with Rob. Not wishing to intrude on any more of her time he stood up to express appreciation and to dismiss himself. But before he left he posed this question: "What advice might you have to offer a young preacher?"

"Only this," she said. "Preach Jesus, the true Jesus, the real Jesus, the resurrected Jesus, and not a Jesus of people's imaginations."

I often get the feeling that people are following a Jesus of their imagination and not the real Jesus, the risen Lord of the universe. Nowhere is this more apparent than in this passage of Scripture. A man comes up to Jesus and makes a bold declaration of allegiance. "I will follow you wherever you go!" Jesus responds by showing this person the concrete reality of what this obedience will entail. "Even the foxes have dens and the birds nests, but the Son of Man is committed to an itinerant lifestyle. Can you really make that kind of commitment?"

My wife and I could hardly wait to receive our first full-time appointment after seminary. We went to meet the Pastor-Parish Committee with great anticipation. The interview went well as each of us had a chance to share our dreams and visions for ministry. There was a real inner affirmation that God had his hand in this appointment. The committee told Carolyn and me that they would be renting an apartment for us to live in, but until that time we would be living with an elderly widower in the church. For the next six weeks we lived in an upstairs attic with a squeaky bed, a picnic table, and a rocking chair.

I remember lying in bed that Saturday night before my first Sunday in my new appointment thinking about these words of Jesus. "The Son of Man has an itinerant lifestyle—follow me!" What a privilege we have in being able to participate in this great adventure. A word of caution. This itinerant lifestyle is not for pastors only. This challenge is for all who call Jesus Lord!

Jesus commands another to follow. This person, like Moses, confuses a decree with a suggestion. The

man really comes up with a good excuse. I have been
a pastor for 20 years and I have heard a lot of excuses,
but his is the best. "Lord, first let me go and bury my
father." He even uses the title "Lord" in referring to
Jesus but obviously does not understand the magni-
tude of its meaning.

Jesus is quick, almost coldly cruel in elevating this
man's understanding: "Let the dead bury their own
dead, but you go and proclaim the kingdom of God."
Jesus is the absolute authority. There is no excuse for
anything other than radical, absolute obedience.

Many of us have a warehouse full of reasons why
we are less than what Christ calls us to be. We often
say that Jesus is first in our lives, but in reality he
comes after careers, relationships, clubs, golf outings,
band practice, football, baseball, soccer, and even yard
work. That is why I am convinced that most people in
the church today are following a Jesus of their imagination and not the risen Lord of the universe.

Another wants to follow, but with a condition.
"First let me go back and say good-bye to my family."
We cannot follow Jesus with any conditional clauses
attached. "No one who puts a hand to the plow and
looks back is fit for the kingdom of God " (Luke 9:62).

In our denomination's tradition the membership
vow is powerful! "Do you accept Jesus Christ as your
Lord and Savior and do you pledge your allegiance to
his kingdom?" The conviction that Jesus is Lord has
been the key theological factor of every awakening.
God is a vague philosophical idea until I meet God
face-to-face in the person of Jesus Christ. Jesus does
not allow me to create a god in my own image who
serves me and my particular prejudices.

As I face Jesus and understand his authority I
must deal with my own self-absorption. Like Zac-
chaeus, the tax collector, I realize that I have a great
responsibility to others if I am going to be in relationship with Jesus (Luke 19:1-9). Like the woman caught

in adultery, I hear Jesus' words of both a full pardon
and the necessity of moral living (John 8: 1-11). Following Jesus involves everything. He is not just one part
of life—he is life! "Do you pledge your allegiance to his
kingdom?" That means your allegiance to Jesus Christ
and his kingdom must supersede any and all other
allegiances in your life.

I have two friends who took this vow very seri-
ously. Tom and Elaine Sampley discovered a personal
relationship with Christ and became very active in
ministry at Ginghamsburg while we were still a very
small church. Like most babyboomers, they were
focused on raising their children and fulfilling their
material and relational needs. I first met Tom and
Elaine in the lean years. Tom was working two jobs
while trying to establish a fledgling real estate business. Long hours and tight finances made for the
typical home tensions. After several years of hard
work Tom and Elaine began to experience financial
success. They built their dream home, complete with
swimming pool, in a prestigious neighborhood.

They had lived in their new home for less than a
year when Tom shared with a small group of men
that met together every Thursday morning about a
new sense of calling: "Would you guys pray for me? I
really don't understand what is going on. But I believe
God wants me to go into full-time ministry."

We prayed and we listened. Tom and Elaine sold
their business, their dream home, and at age 45, set off
for Bible school. They spent the next two years ex-
hausting their resources on tuition, living expenses,
and the tuition of their two older children still in
college. Today Tom is the admissions director of The
Word of Life Bible Center in Schroon Lake, New York.
Remember:

> We do not live to ourselves, and we do not die
> to ourselves. If we live, we live to the Lord, and
> if we die, we die to the Lord; so then, whether

we live or whether we die, we are the Lord's.
For to this end Christ died and lived again, so
that he might be Lord of both the dead and the
living (Romans 14: 7-9).

The Good New About Jesus

Philip was traveling the desert road south from
Jerusalem to Gaza. On the way he met an Ethiopian
eunuch who was on official business for the queen.
The Ethiopian had been reading from the book of
Isaiah. Philip took advantage of the situation and,
beginning at the passage from which the Ethiopian
had been reading, "he proclaimed to him the good
news about Jesus" (Acts 8:35).

Telling the good news about Jesus is the unique
business of the church. The YMCA has excellent
camping and recreation programs. There are many
effective social service agencies in our communities.
Multitudes of clubs and organizations welcome our
people's participation and involvement. We can offer
those around us only one thing that these organizations do not already offer—JESUS CHRIST. We must be
careful not to water down the message with a vague
theism.

Jesus Christ said, "And I, when I am lifted up from
the earth, will draw all people to myself" (John 12:32).
In my preaching, teaching, counseling, and administration at Ginghamsburg church I have sought to do
this one thing—lift up Jesus Christ. Renewal theology
reduced to the least complicated denominator is
simply lifting up Jesus in every act of the church.
When Jesus becomes the focus of the life of the local
church, new life comes to dry bones and people begin
to stand up on their feet and become a vital army.

Notes

1 Lyle E. Schaller, "What Happened to Denominations," *Church Management, The Clergy Journal,* October, 1992, 45-47.

2 Hugh T. Kerr and John M. Mulder, Editors, *Conversions: The Christian Experience,* Eerdmans Publishing Co., Grand Rapids, Michigan, 1983, 11.

3 F. J. Foakes-Jackson, *History of the Christian Church to A.D. 461,* W. P. Blessing, Chicago, 1927, 494.

4 Foakes-Jackson, 495.

5 A. G. Dickens, *The Counter-Reformation,* Harcourt, Brace & World, Inc., Great Britain, 1969, 37.

6 Roland Bainton, *Here I Stand: A Life of Martin Luther,* Abingdon-Cokesbury Press, New York, Nashville, 1950, 60.

7 Dickens, 7.

8 Dickens, 77, 80.

9 Nehemiah Curnock, ed., *The Journal of John Wesley,* Eaton and Mains, New York, 1909, 471-72.

10 Curnock, 475-76.

11 Curnock, 477-78.

12 Robert W. Burtner and Robert E. Chiles, *A Compend of Wesley's Theology,* Abingdon Press, New York, Nashville, 1954, 73.

*Scriptural Truth
as the Primary Source
for what we Believe and Do*

Chapter Two

When the king heard the words of the book of the law, he tore his clothes. Then the king commanded the priest Hilkiah Ahikam son of Shaphan, Achbor son of Micaiah, Shaphan the secretary, and the king's servant Asaiah, saying, "Go, inquire of the LORD for me, for the people, and for all Judah, concerning the words of this book that has been found; for great is the wrath of the LORD that is kindled against us, because our ancestors did not obey the words of this book, to do according to all that is written concerning us" (2 Kings 22:11-13).

Getting Back to the Book

Josiah was born during the last half of the seventh century B.C., during the reign of the corrupt king Manasseh. It was probably the lowest, darkest moment in Israel's history. For years the people had been assimilating the pagan practices of the surrounding cultures and disregarding God's command to remain separate and distinct. Preceding kings of Judah had even accepted the practice of sun worship.

Manasseh surpassed them all. He imported pagan priests and established male cult prostitutes throughout the countryside. Pagan deities and images were erected in the temple. Offerings were made to Baal and to the female fertility goddess Asherah. Human sacrifices were being made in the Hinnom Valley to the pagan god Molech. Manasseh even sank to the despicable act of sacrificing his own son in the fire (2 Kings 21). The people were turning to mediums and spiritualists for guidance. Household gods and idols flourished. God's people were adrift in a sea of spiritual and moral confusion. The clear call of the God of Abraham, Isaac, and Jacob was no longer heard.

A voice of reformation cried out from the ashes. Josiah, who became the boy king of Judah at the age of eight, would be God's agent for renewal.

> He did what was right in the sight of the LORD, and walked in the ways of his ancestor David; he did not turn aside to the right or to the left. For in the eighth year of his reign, while he was still a boy, he began to seek the God of his ancestor David ... (2 Chronicles 34:2-3).

During the early years of his reign Josiah began a series of sweeping reforms. He tore down the regional altars of sacrifice and attempted to restore the temple as the central place of worship. He worked at purging the pagan influences that had been assimilated into the faith. The altars of the Baals, Asherah poles, idols and images were smashed to pieces. The corrupt priests were removed.

Josiah turned his attention to the repair and reform of the temple in Jerusalem when he was 26 years old. A crucial discovery was made during these repairs. It was a discovery that has been essential to every renewal of God's people. While the workers were restoring the temple, an old, dusty, misplaced book was found by Hilkiah, the high priest. It was the Book of the Law of the Lord that had been given through Moses. Its vital message had gone unheard by the people for decades. The Mosaic Book of the Law was brought to King Josiah. When he heard the words of the book he realized that Judah had drastically deviated from God's plan. They had been a people building without a blueprint. Josiah had the people gather at the temple to hear the words of the book that had been found on a dusty shelf. The result was radical revitalization! The people turned from dead institutionalism to the living God.

The Standard for Faith

Renewal grows out of rediscovery of biblical truth. The church rediscovers the lost book and reaffirms the unique, timeless revelation that God has made through its transforming message. The Bible becomes the standard for faith in the midst of a sea of voices crying to be heard in the philosophical and moral wilderness.

What happened to Judah also reoccurs throughout church history. Martin Luther discovered the lost book out of a sense of frustration with the tired, shifting traditions of the church. He experienced the voice of God through the book of Romans. His *Sola Scriptura* approach to the faith fanned the flames of the Reformation. Luther translated the Bible into the common language of the masses, which inspired both Protestant and Catholic reformations.

Nearly 200 years later, John Wesley heard God's voice while attending a Moravian Bible study group. They were studying Luther's notes on the book of Romans. Wesley's life, and the lives of millions of others influenced by his teachings, would never again be the same. He became "a man of one book." For Wesley, the Bible was the last word in determining the boundaries of the Christian faith.

> The Christian rule of right and wrong is the Word of God, the writings of the Old and New Testament; all that the prophets and "holy men of old" wrote "as they were moved by the Holy Ghost"; all that Scripture which was "given by inspiration of God," and which is indeed "profitable for doctrine," or teaching the

whole will of God; "for reproof" of what is
contrary thereto; for "correction" of error; and
"for instruction," or training us up, "in righ-
teousness" (2 Tim. 3:16). This is a lantern unto
a Christian's feet, and a light in all his paths.
This alone he receives as his rule of right or
wrong, of whatever is really good or evil.[1]

Wesley held Scripture above reason, experience
and tradition in determining Christian truth. He saw
Scripture as the final testing ground of authenticity.

My ground is the Bible. Yea, I am a Bible-bigot.
I follow it in all things, both great and small.
In matters of religion I regard no writings but
the inspired. Touler, Behmen, and an whole
army of mystic authors are with me nothing
to St. Paul. In every point I appeal "to the law
and the testimony," and value no authority but
this.[2]

Robert Chiles writes:

He [Wesley] was well acquainted with and
drew upon the early church fathers and the
lessons of church history. He was particularly
attentive to those factors that he believed had
obscured and distorted the realities of primitive Christianity. He held that the great coun-
cils of the church were subject to error, and he
insisted on checking their pronouncements
against the Scriptures. In this, as in all things,
Wesley contended that the written Word of
God stand as the sole authority for Christians
and the church.[3]

Beyond Opinions

Week after week countless numbers of our
people slumber through our sermons. Pastors often

wonder why parishioners are critical or indifferent toward their preaching and bemoan sermons that last longer than 15 or 20 minutes.

People are longing for a word from God. They are not interested in our personal opinions. They want more than the latest book review or political commentary. Our people yearn for a message from God in an age of uncertainty and materialistic self-centeredness. In a time when the nuclear family is being redefined through divorce and single parenting, does God still speak with a voice of hope? In an age of global political and economic instability, growing racial tension, uncertain moral boundaries and AIDS—is there a word from God?

Have you ever wondered why so many people were willing to follow a nonconformist, upstart preacher like John the Baptist into the wilderness? John could have been accused of not having both oars in the water. He was eccentric. Not many people of his day wore animal skins or observed his dietary habits. He did not have the best pastoral attitude, calling people "brood of vipers" and the like.

Yet John preached to standing-room-only crowds in the desert, and there was no air conditioning! It was not for a lack of religious leaders. Jerusalem was full of liberal and conservative teachers well versed in their religious opinions and theological jargons. John did not even have formal theological training. But he spoke with a different kind of authority. He did not say "I think" or "I believe" or "I feel." John spoke with the authority of the Word of God.

Faith Comes from Hearing

Our people have become biblically illiterate. They are no longer "a people of one book." For many the Bible is a filing system for sacred family treasures that are stored between its pages. It is hidden away on

a shelf or ornamentally displayed on a table. In our
Sunday school classes we study books about the Book
or hear stories from the Book, but we rarely study the
Book. Our pastors have lost the art of relevant biblical
preaching. Many see the Bible as a collection of non-
related ancient books that are irrelevant to our highly
complex technological society. They fail to see the
amazing interrelatedness of these books that tell one
story. It is the story of paradise lost and paradise re-
gained. It is the message of God's far reaching and
never failing love. It is a history of personal victory
and hope. It is the promise of purpose and direction
through Jesus Christ.

My formative years fell during the 1960s when
many of the young people my age were looking for
answers to very real problems. I grew up in a fairly
typical mainline church. It was neither hot nor cold.
My family rarely missed worship or Sunday school. I
remember studying the book *Catcher in the Rye* in
my freshman Sunday-school class with a teacher who
claimed to be agnostic. My church was offering no
prophetic messages of hope or purpose.

Like many my age, I was greatly influenced by
the British music invasion that came with the Beatles.
My parents gave me my first guitar when I was in the
eighth grade. By my junior year in high school the
band that I played in managed our own teen club. My
highest grade that year was a "D." I finished the year
with two "Fs" and three "Ds." Things only got worse
during my senior year. Two of the guys in the group
were arrested for possession of drugs. One of my
teachers changed an "F" to a "D minus" less than a
week before graduation, which allowed me to graduate with my class.

Out of a sense of desperation I began to ask some
pretty basic questions: "Is there a God?" "Is God good?"
"What is God like?" "Does God care for me?" One night,
either out of boredom or in a desperate search for

purpose, I pulled out a dust-covered book from the stand next to my bed. It was the Bible I had been given in my third-grade Sunday-school class. For some reason I skipped over the Old Testament and went right to the Gospel stories. I probably would have quit prematurely if I had started in Genesis or Leviticus. As I began the nightly ritual of reading from this book, something strange began to happen in my life. I found a magnetic attraction to the person of Jesus. "Is this what God is like?" I asked myself. I could hardly believe the words of Jesus that I read in John 8 concerning the woman who was caught in adultery, "Neither do I condemn you."

"Is it possible," I thought to myself, "that God's love and forgiveness are this broad? Could it be that God's goodness extends to those who are caught red-handed? And what is this? Jesus is the friend of sinners! He travels with undesirables. He invites prostitutes to be his friends. This is too good to be true! This means that there is hope for me."

There was something radically different about the man in these stories. He even got into hassles with religious people. (We do seem to be the source of many of the problems in the church.) I could not wait to read more about him each night. After all my years in the church, I was seeing the uniqueness of Jesus for the first time. It was not an overnight experience. I did not know any terminology like "born again." But somehow I deeply sensed that life's purpose could be found in him. I knew that Christ and Christ alone held the key to what I was yearning for deep within my spirit.

Confrontation with the Word of God awakens faith. "So faith comes from what is heard, and what is heard comes through the word of Christ" (Romans 10:17). As we are exposed to the words of this book our spirit bears witness with God's Spirit to the reality of life found in Christ.

The Scripture does not bear witness to itself. It does not call us to believe in Scripture, it calls us to believe in the One whom God has sent.

> Now Jesus did many other signs in the presence of his disciples, which are not written in this book. But these are written so that you may come to believe that Jesus is the Messiah, the Son of God, and that through believing you may have life in his name (John 20:30-31).

The Bible is the word of God with the small "w" that points us to the living Word of God with the capital "W." The focus is not the Bible, it is Christ! The Bible is not an end in itself but a means to an end, which is life in Christ.

When the Ethiopian eunuch asked Philip to explain a passage of Scripture from Isaiah, Philip did not give him a long cerebral theological discourse. He didn't say: "Oh, I am glad you asked. Isaiah was really written by two different authors at two different points in history. So there is really a first and a second Isaiah. The author was probably symbolically referring to historical events of his time period and not intentionally aware of the prophetic implications." The eunuch would have either been confused or asleep by the time Philip had finished the second sentence.

Philip did not take the other approach of focusing on the Scripture as an end in itself. "I am so glad you have a Bible and you are reading it. Believe it, young man. It is the word of God. Believe it. Read it. And you will never go wrong."

Philip was wise. He understood the importance of the written word for what it is. "Then Philip began to speak, and starting with this scripture, he proclaimed to him the good news about Jesus" (Acts 8:35). He did not give the eunuch information. He gave him Jesus. The purpose of Scripture is not information—it is transformation in Christ.

We have been trained in our seminaries to approach the Scriptures from a historical-critical perspective. Our heads have been stuffed full of information that we bring back to our people, but information does not give life. I have visited many Sunday school classes where the people were going through their quarterlies studying the life of Abraham, Moses, David or one of the other biblical characters. Information is given about 4000-year-old people and we feel that the purpose of the class has been accomplished. Scripture was not given for information. It was given that we might see the one who is the author of life and be radically transformed through him.

We find Christ in the Scripture as we can in no other way. Luke records these words of Jesus to his disciples after the Resurrection:

> "These are my words that I spoke to you while I was still with you—that everything written about me in the law of Moses, the prophets, and the psalms must be fulfilled." Then he opened their minds to understand the scriptures ... (Luke 24:44-45).

The disciples had grown up steeped in the history, tradition and information of the Scriptures. Jesus took them past the information to the place of understanding—the place of transformation.

Doers of the Word

> But be doers of the word, and not merely hearers who deceive themselves (James 1:22).

Isaiah was ministering in Judah when the people were going through a "heightened-religious-interest" phase. The people were returning to the temple in great numbers. There was a resurgence of emphasis on personal piety. People were praying and fasting again. Bible study, family values and personal moral-

ity were the order of the day. Some would have called
what was happening "renewal." The people were
attending Bible studies and filling their notebooks
full of information—but they stopped short of transformation. They wondered why God didn't hear their
prayers.

God tells Judah through the prophet Isaiah that
true renewal demonstrates itself in our relationships
with people. People moved by God's Spirit will be
involved with the oppressed, hungry and homeless
poor. People who are informed by the Word of God
will be held accountable for living the whole justice
of God.

> Is not this the fast that I choose: to loose the
> bonds of injustice, to undo the thongs of the
> yoke, to let the oppressed go free, and to break
> every yoke? Is it not to share your bread with
> the hungry, and bring the homeless poor into
> your house; when you see the naked, to cover
> them, and not to hide yourself from your own
> kin? Then your light shall break forth like the
> dawn, and your healing shall spring up quick-
> ly (Isaiah 58: 6-8).

During the fall of 1979 the people of Ginghamsburg church decided that we needed to be practicing
what we were learning from God's Word. It was clear
that renewal and involvement with hurting people
had a direct correlation. We started the "adopt-a-
Christmas family" program, which involved the
commitment to spend on a family in need the same
amount that you would spend on your own family.
Many of us in the past had simply gone to the local
discount store and spent five dollars or less on a cheap
toy or pair of mittens, wrapped them and then
dropped the package in a barrel in the hallway of the
church. Or worse yet, some have brought an old doll

from home, one with crayon marks and half the hair missing, and given it in the name of Christian love. Let's be honest. This is not love—it is cleaning out the garage.

The leading of the Spirit was clear. If you bought your child a new bike, you would buy another child a new bike. Why was a used bike good enough for someone else's child if it wasn't good enough for your own? If a used bicycle was good enough for your boy or girl, then it was okay to give one to another. If you bought your child name-brand clothes, then you would buy another child name-brand clothes.

We were all assigned names and went to meet our "adopted" families around Thanksgiving. The shopping adventure began as we set out with names, sizes and wish lists. Most of us delivered our gifts on Christmas Eve.

When we all assembled in our little red-brick-and-frame country church for the 11 p.m. candlelight service you could sense a feeling of euphoria. As we sang our Christmas carols we knew that we had truly acted Christian!

Do you know what God had the nerve to say to us?

> "You hypocrites. How dare you think that you are loving with the love of my Son when you love with sacrificial love only one day out of 365. If you are truly my disciples you will be involved with these people 365 days a year."

> "What are you saying, Lord? 365 days? Lord, that means that they will have to have my telephone number."

That is exactly what it means! Loving with Christ's love means that when I buy my kids' back-to-school clothes I will buy my Christmas family back-to-school clothes also. When I send my two kids to camp, I will send my Christmas-family kids to camp. When our daughter, Kristen, had braces put on her teeth we made the commitment to help a young college student get braces. This lifestyle of giving can be pretty scary. My son just got braces!

Renewal broke out at our church when the people began actively to do what we had been reading in God's written word. Jesus was taking us past the information to the place of transformation.

My good friends Tom and Lisa Jelenek came to Ginghamsburg shortly after they were married in 1983. Tom is an environment specialist with a large company and Lisa teaches French at one of the area high schools. Tom made a commitment to Jesus as Savior and Lord during his first year at Ginghamsburg and both began to grow in Christian discipleship.

Through their newly discovered practice of Bible reading they began to develop a deeper sense of responsibility toward meeting the needs of others. Tom became deeply involved in our mission outreach programs. Many of our mission ministries began under Tom's direction. One Thanksgiving he worked with a mission team to rebuild houses in South Carolina following Hurricane Hugo.

Lisa began a friendship with Karen, a woman who had been in and out of several disastrous marriages, the victim of abuse and co-dependent relationships since childhood. Tom and Lisa helped Karen become reestablished in a new apartment. They welcomed her often into their home, brought her to church and helped her get through nursing school. Why?

"I just couldn't help it," Lisa said. "It was the Holy Spirit, Mike. When I looked at this woman who had been abused by her husband and had no where to go . . . I just had to help. I looked at everything we had and the very little that she had. The Spirit helped me get beyond my materialistic lifestyle to reach out to someone in need."

It is the business of the church to enable people to come to this point of biblical understanding that results in transformation. This was my first priority when I came to Ginghamsburg church. I encourage the people to bring their Bibles to worship. We look at the different passages together. The people make notes, underline and ask questions. The Bible has become the chief source once again in our Sunday school classes. I have taught the Trinity Bible Study series on Wednesday nights since 1982. As our people become more exposed to the message of this unique book, they become more focused in their commitment to Christ and his church. They move out of the pew and on to the playing field. Rugged individualism and self-centeredness are replaced with a sense of true community. Dead organizations become living organisms. Closed minds give way to the mind of Christ. Prejudice and judgment yield to justice and active love.

Renewal depends upon the local church rediscovering the vital, unique truth that God has given us in this book. The Scripture must be seen as the primary source for determining all matters of faith and practice in our spiritual journeys. As St. John of the Cross has so aptly stated, "If we are guided by divine Scripture we shall not be able to err, for he who speaks in it is the Holy Ghost."[4]

Notes

1 Robert Wallace Burtner and Robert Eugene Chiles, *A Compend of Wesley's Theology,* Abingdon Press, New York, Nashville, 1954, 21.

2 Burtner and Chiles, 20, 21.

3 Robert E. Chiles, *Scriptural Christianity: A Call to John Wesley's Disciples,* Francis Asbury Press, Zondervan Corp., Grand Rapids, Michigan, 1984, 70.

4 A. G. Dickens, *The Counter Reformation,* Harcourt, Brace, and World, Inc., Great Britain, 1969, 160.

The Liturgical PRINCIPLE

Discovery of
New Worship Forms

Chapter Three

You can batten down ... just like a voice echoing through a cave ... you can enjoy your classic worship in this cathedral. But this is not where this culture is. The Spirit of God is moving out there.

Dr. Leonard Sweet
United Theological Seminary

Martin Luther was sitting in a German beer garden surrounded by baskets of red and white geraniums hanging from wooden beams. The tables were occupied by college students who had evaded their afternoon classes to find refreshment in the midst of the afternoon heat. He looked with deep passion into faces of these young people who had so quickly neglected the eternal for the sake of temporal economic dreams and humanistic philosophies. He contemplated ways to bridge the cavernous gap between the message of Jesus and the cultural identity of these students.

On this particular humid afternoon the students seemed to be in an especially good mood as they sang a college fraternity song and lifted their mugs of hefeweizen beer. Luther listened intently. Walking home through the street lined with red-roofed houses, he couldn't seem to get the melody of that tune out of his head. He would repeatedly find himself humming it. "That's it!" It was as if the idea came directly from heaven.

Luther was so concerned with finding ways of reaching those young college students that he put the gospel message into popular-music form. Historians are not certain whether Luther composed the tune for the hymn "A Mighty Fortress Is Our God," but it is well documented that many of Luther's hymns were inspired by the "beer-garden" music forms of his day.

> [Luther's] tunes were largely made up from phrases from plainsong or adaptations of current songs, some of which were already associated with sacred words and some with secular. He was chided for going so far afield as to bring folk songs into the sanctuary. . . . And the practical effect of Luther's course was not to secularize church song so much as to turn the current of German music into a religious channel. . . . The twice-told tale of his phenomenal success in making popular song his agent in spreading the gospel and heartening the gospelers does not need to be repeated here.[1]

Renewal gives birth to new worship forms that relate to the needs and culture of unchurched people rather than the preferences of the churched. Jesus said he came to "seek and save what was lost" (Luke 19:10). This mission becomes the primary focus of both the church and forms of worship in renewal.

Relating to the Needs of the Unchurched

John Wesley was comfortable in the high church setting and was committed to his formal, liturgical Anglican background. This presented a rather complex dilemma when the pulpits of the Church of England began to close to him because of his newly found experience in Christ and his emphasis on salvation by faith. He found his audience almost by default to be made up primarily of the unchurched working class. It didn't take Wesley long to see that the traditional way of doing things wasn't going to work. The liturgy and hymnody were irrelevant to the unchurched crowds who would often jeer and shout obscenities. Some would stop and briefly listen but Wesley could not seem to keep their attention long enough to reach their hearts with the gospel.

John said to his brother Charles, "Chuck, the German music is too heavy and not melodic enough for the English coal miner. Go out and listen to the workers sing their music as they go back and forth to the mines and then sit down and write something that will reach their hearts."

Charles Wesley's work put the gospel message into a "Top 40" format. He wrote "folk music" for the sake of relating the gospel to the hearts of the unchurched masses. He felt that his music was not "reverent" enough to be used in the formal worship of the church but intended it to be used only for the informal house meetings. The institutional church of his day never accepted his style.

The Methodist renewal was born out of the contemporary music forms of Wesley's day. As the gospel becomes relevant to the unchurched through their own indigenous cultural forms they begin to flood the church to the extent that they become more numerous than the churched. The informal then replaces the formal and becomes the new liturgical form. This is a critical renewal principle. The church always adopts the worship forms of the last renewal movement. The church is currently using worship forms that are 125-255 years old. We may update the words and images in the new *Book of Worship,* but the wineskins are still old and brittle. It is time to get new wineskins to hold new wine.

Wesley's goal was to reach the hearts of the unchurched people. That's also the agenda of Jesus. Jesus didn't come to cater to the preferences of the church goers. He came to meet the needs of the unchurched. This must be our agenda, too!

Worship That Makes Sense

We were created to worship. Worship is that place where we get in touch with God's presence and discover anew who we are. Through worship our spirits are energized and priorities realigned. Worship is meant to be at the heart of life, but has often been presented in a way that is divorced from life.

I was speaking in a large major denomination, church recently. During the worship time I saw boredom and indifference written all over the faces of yawning people. Many were just going through the motions of reciting ancient, tired rituals. Up, down. Up, down. "Didn't we just sit down?" wonders a mother as she wrestles with her struggling two-year-old and tries to juggle her bulletin and hymnal. Somehow the Apostles' Creed does not seem relevant to the moment.

I know these yawning people get excited about other things. I have witnessed their zealous enthusiasm at athletic events, Rotary clubs and sales meetings. Yet we can be so apathetic about worship. We wonder where our young people have gone. Most of our churches are perceived as offering worship that is irrelevant to our everyday lives. The worship bulletin may announce that the organ prelude is "Preghiera in E" by Oresta Ravenello, but what difference does that make? People are looking for something fresh and vital. The worship experience must make sense to them.

In my first year of ministry at the Ginghamsburg church I was visiting the home of one of our older members who was convinced that the contemporary music we were using on Sunday morning was "inap-

propriate for God's house." He was passionately pleading the case for adhering to the sacred hymnody and
traditions of the church.

"Pastor," he said as he cleared his voice, "how can
God be happy with this hippity hop music? People
even want to clap their hands. It just isn't being re-
spectful to God to clap in church."

I happened to notice that he had quite an extensive record collection and asked what he might have
in the way of sacred hymns. His response didn't sur-
prise me. He was an avid collector of the big band era
with such names as Benny Goodman, Stan Kenton,
George Getz and Duke Ellington, but he didn't have a
single album of sacred hymnody in this collection! He
was pleading the cause of the importance of the
traditional hymns, but his collection betrayed his
first love in music.

Why do we cling to worship forms that are so
formal when our everyday lives are so informal?
Sometimes we try to force on others what doesn't
even work for us. Many of our theological terms and
phrases do not make sense to unchurched people. For
them, sitting through a worship service is like listening to the technological jargon of a rocket propulsion
expert or a surgeon. Worship must relate to the nitty-
gritty places of ordinary people in everyday life. We
cannot make sense of what we have not experienced.

As our American pioneer culture moved westward, the Methodists and Baptists were masters at
relating the gospel to a resistant unchurched culture.
They were instrumental in the Second Great Awakening because of their effective use of hard-hitting,
relevant preaching, common-sense worship and
upbeat music. Peter Cartwright, one of the great
frontier preachers, claimed:

> ... the great mass of our western people
> wanted a preacher that could mount a stump,
> a block, or old log, or stand in the bed of a

wagon, and without note or manuscript, quote, expound, and apply the word of God to the hearts and consciences of the people.[2]

The music and worship forms of the rapidly growing frontier church were vastly different from the eastern churches that held to highly institutional and formal services. The music was essentially "folk" music. The worship "was crude and direct."[3] This make-sense approach of frontier worship that was directed at the heart of an unchurched audience is one of the primary reasons we find Baptist or Methodist churches in most of the counties in the United States.

Worship is one of the most important experiences that we have together as a community of faith. It must be vital and relevant to people in the context of their life situations. We have to work hard at not letting it become drab, routine or boring.

Vital Worship

At the Ginghamsburg church we assemble worship teams comprised of people who play synthesizers, guitars, flutes, horns, cellos, drums and a variety of other instruments. Not only does this better reflect the music of our contemporary culture but it gives many more people an opportunity to participate in worship using their gifts and talents. How many baby boomers have a guitar tucked away in a closet somewhere? One of our Sunday school classes is for people interested in playing in the church orchestra. Another is for the youth praise team. These classes attract people by their interests and make wise use of time for people with very hectic lifestyles.

We talk about worship and evaluate worship every week as a leadership team. It is very important that the celebration of worship doesn't become predictable and routine. Nontraditional orders of wor-

ship can just as quickly fall into the rut of predictabil-
ity as more traditional styles. We make use of creative
calls to worship, drama, times of prayer and opportunities for people to share personal expressions about
their faith journeys. It is important to use a variety of
prayer experiences including conversational prayer
and small group prayer circles. The people of God
will never learn to be the priesthood of God if all we
ever use are pastoral prayers.

People need to be players and not spectators in
the worship experience. On occasion I have begun
worship by asking the people to call us to worship by
sharing with the congregation significant Scripture
passages that they found particularly meaningful
during the previous week. People will then stand up
in the midst of the gathering and share a brief verse
or two. The worship team, made up of 8 to 20 members, then leads us in a time of worship and praise. We
usually sing from four to six songs. The first song is
usually very celebrative and upbeat. The last is soft
and reflective. This time of worship might include a
traditional hymn more often than not done in an
untraditional way.

This time of worship is usually followed by a
period of prayer. The prayer might be conversational,
or an individual might be called on to lead the time
of prayer. The prayer time might have a theme such
as thanksgiving, confession or intercession. Sometimes we pray for those who express particular needs.

Personal faith stories help build faith. We often
have a time of sharing in our order of worship for this
purpose. Sometimes people are encouraged to stand
and briefly share their witness from their seat. We
also have people share their testimonies, with ad-
vance notice, from the pulpit. Brevity must be considered. We ask the people who share their testimony
from the pulpit to write it out first and limit it to
three minutes. A staff person listens and helps them

make adjustments ahead of time. We do not want to
appear slick, but we are committed to excellence.

A time of sharing is followed by skits, special
music, offering, ministry of the Word and benedic-
tion. Sometimes the closing experience offers the
people a moment to share "what I am hearing God say
to me through this experience." The total worship
celebration lasts between 60 and 70 minutes.

I cannot overstate the importance of allowing
worship to be unpredictable and people-involved.

"Your worship experience should not be totally
dependent upon me," I shared with the people at the
opening of one of the worship celebrations. "The
Bible says that each person should bring a unique gift
to offer to God in the worship experience. One can
bring a hymn, another share a prayer. Someone else
can offer a word of testimony."

I wasn't sure that it was going to work. With
hesitancy and reservation about the potential negative fallout, I struck out for the unpredictable yet
potentially promising learning experience.

"I am going to leave worship right now and go
back and take care of the kids in the nursery."

Silence was the only response I heard as I stepped
off the platform and made my way down the aisle
and out the back doors of the small sanctuary. Would
chaos ensue? I wondered to myself. Will the visitors
come back? Will I still have a job next Sunday? I listened intently to the small speaker box on the nursery wall that carried the sounds of a murmuring
audience from the sanctuary. It's not going to work.
Now what? The thought was interrupted by a familiar
voice. It was the voice of Deane Loar that I heard
through the speaker box on the wall.

"I know that you all might think this is silly, but I
make up songs in the shower. Songs that are for God."

With that Deane began to sing a song for the
congregation that he had written for God. Then he

taught them to sing it. It was simple, but the impact was humbling and powerful.

Len Kubal then came forward and read a particularly meaningful passage of Scripture that had confronted him during the week. Tom Sampley shared about the devastating loss of his brother. The people ministered to him in prayer.

I didn't preach that weekend, but it is probably the most powerful message that I have ever delivered.

All this change didn't occur at once. I began to use my guitar in worship when the organist quit. It was by accident that I first discovered the impact contemporary music would have in worship! I was at Ginghamsburg seven years before worship teams were fully incorporated into our worship experience.

Communion is celebrated the first Sunday of every month along with the invitation to prayer and the anointing with oil for those with needs for healing. These vehicles of grace have often been overlooked or downplayed in the church. We need to discover the presence of Christ anew through them.

Worship and Word

We must be sensitive to the "user-friendly" models of worship that are growing in popularity without compromising the radical demands of the call of Christ in the name of relevancy. I often hear people say that they were attracted to Ginghamsburg church because of the contemporary style of worship and preaching.

People are looking for a relevant word but not a compromising word. They are listening for a clear word from God in the midst of a labyrinth of theological and moral uncertainty. The churches with relevant worship styles, Christ-centered prophetic preaching and social sensitivity will offer new life and hope to this age.

What Makes Worship Vital?

What attracts people to a worship celebration? Why do they want to return? What makes worship vital? These are some of the responses from people when asked about their worship experience at Ginghamsburg church.

- "The very first time I entered this church I had the feeling that something was different, something I never experienced in any other church. I couldn't put my finger on what this difference was right away. It wasn't until we became part of the church some months later that I realized that what I was experiencing for the first time was the Holy Spirit in action through the people there. They would love us. It was just a rather unusual feeling that I experienced the very first time that I came here."

- "We came in and it was kind of noisy and there was a lot of life and there were lots of people talking to each other and, from my experience, a little bit of chaos."

- "I saw people hugging each other. After church people were standing around talking. That wasn't the type of church that I had gone to where people left immediately after church was over."

- "I think informal worship has definitely made an impact on my worship experience because there is a freedom there that allows the Holy Spirit to just work in me."

- "It is exhilarating for us to come together and collectively acknowledge Jesus as Lord. The testimonies of others heal me. I walk away and say 'Yes, Lord, it's exciting to see how you are using your people.' The opportunity to just share life with each other in his presence is part of worship here."

Notice the emphasis placed upon worship that is experiential and relational rather than worship that is informational and ritualistic. Words frequently used to describe worship include experience, feeling, experiencing the Holy Spirit, action, love, relationships, hugging, talking, enjoying, freedom, exhilarating, collectively, testimonies, healing, exciting, sharing life, in his presence. These people are talking about experiencing God and celebrating his presence as they celebrate and experience real life.

We are more than cerebral beings. We are whole persons. Vital worship must speak to the whole of human experience. It must reach into the physical, spiritual, relational, emotional, and rational dimensions of who we are as the people of Jesus in a real world context. This type of worship continually calls us back to authentic living under the lordship of Jesus Christ.

What Would You Do If You Were in St. Pete?

A friend of mine, who also happened to be a district superintendent, was visiting one of our three worship celebrations on a Sunday morning. He noticed immediately the informal dress of the predominantly baby-boomer-age congregation as he entered the multipurpose room that already had well over 400 people in a space designed for 270. The room was vibrating with conversation, laughter and anticipation. He sensed what some have described as a mild atmosphere of chaos as people maneuvered their way through the crowd to get a cup of coffee and ushers moved with intention and efficiency in creating extra space. He couldn't help but notice the enthusiasm and participation of the people in the worship experience as contrasted to most of the churches in his district.

"Mike, I know this worship style is working for you," he commented. "But look at your congregation.

It is so young. You have done a great job in reaching the baby-boomer generation in your geographical area. But what would you do if you were in an area where most of the people were older? What style of worship would you offer if you lived in a retirement area, like St. Petersburg, Florida?

"Dick," I replied, "if I lived in an area like St. Pete, I would offer the best Big Band sound on Sunday morning that you ever heard."

The agenda of Jesus is not the preference of the churched, but the needs of the unchurched. If the church is to experience a new movement of the Spirit, we need new worship forms to hold new wine.

Notes

1 Louis F. Benson, *The Hymnody of the Christian Church.* New York: George H. Doran Company, 1927, 240-241.

2 Kenneth G. Phifer, *A Protestant Case for Liturgical Renewal.* Philadelphia: The Westminster Press, 1965, 98.

3 Phifer, 103.

**Commitment to the
Integrity of Membership**

Chapter Four

The church is a covenant community which means that there are gates. You know when you are in and when you are out of the community, even though the Gospel issues a call to everyone. Jesus said, "If anyone would come after me let them deny themselves, take up their cross and follow me." There is a sense in which following Jesus has an element of exclusiveness to it. We decide what not to follow in order to follow Christ, not just individually but as part of the community. Every church has to wrestle with the cost of discipleship as it relates to being a part of this community of Jesus Christ.

Howard Snyder, author, pastor, and seminary professor

It costs something to be a follower of Jesus Christ. It costs something to be committed to his body.

Whenever Jesus' message would begin to attract a large following he would always blow it by saying something incredibly brash and even negative. He had a way of abruptly jarring people into the reality of what following him was all about.

"Whoever comes to me and does not hate father and mother, wife and children, brothers and sisters, yes, and even life itself, cannot be my disciple" (Luke 14:26).

"If any want to become my followers, let them
deny themselves and take up their cross daily
and follow me" (Luke 9:23).

"Foxes have holes, and birds of the air have
nests; but the Son of Man has nowhere to lay
his head" (Luke 9:58).

Are you ready to buy into that kind of itinerant
lifestyle? Do you really understand with whom you
are asking to become involved?

Jesus was always calling people to calculate the
cost. He was not a pop psychologist hawking a gospel
of individualistic positive thinking. He was calling
people to become part of a covenant community, a
counterculture. Membership would involve forsaking
individual goals and agendas for the sake of a higher
purpose—the kingdom of God.

This call upset many of the institutionally religious. The author of the Gospel of John tells us that
many of Jesus' disciples felt that his teaching "is difficult" (John 6:60): "Because of this many of his disciples turned back and no longer went about with
him" (John 6:66).

Many of the churched today see membership in
the church in the same context as membership in a
community club or organization. The church is just
one of several organizations that we are affiliated
with that has officers, committees, dinners, dues and
money-making projects. The church is given equal or
even less priority than other responsibilities in our
lives. Many approach scouting, sports, Rotary club,
golf outings and countless other activities with a
greater zeal and intensity than any activity of the
church.

The Son of God did not give his life for this institutional concept of church membership. It is far more
costly to belong to the body of Christ than any human organization. Like marriage, membership in

Christ's body is a covenant commitment. A covenant is different from institutional membership in the sense that it is unbreakable. Unlike any other commitment we make, membership in Christ's body is an eternal commitment.

The Membership Requirements at Ginghamsburg Church

When a church gets serious about renewal it begins to ask new questions about the responsibilities of membership. Membership cannot and must not be separated from the cost of discipleship. Many people sense there is no cost involved in their local church membership. Not much is expected. It is often harder to get into Cub Scouts than become a member in many of our traditional church settings. At least I had to go out and climb 10 feet up in a tree, acknowledged and signed off by my dad, to begin my journey into scouts. My local church had no real expectations. At most I was handed a box of offering envelopes.

The average attendance exceeds membership at Ginghamsburg by almost 500 people. A typical church in my denomination has a 39% ratio of attendance to membership. Attendance that is lower than the membership is always the sign of a declining church. In renewal, the number of those coming to see what the Spirit of God is doing will always be greater than those who have accepted the commitment of covenant membership.

It costs something to be a follower of Jesus Christ. It costs something to be a member of his Body. When people seek membership with Ginghamsburg church we ask them to spend three months in a class called Vital Christianity (see Appendix A). All missed classes must be made up if they are serious about pursuing membership. Attendance alone, however, does not insure membership. Their commitment to the lord-

ship of Jesus Christ as evidenced by life-style integrity
is a primary consideration. Accepting the responsibilities and commitments of covenant membership
through active stewardship, worship attendance,
participation in a service-outreach ministry and
involvement in a small group is expected. The small
group insures accountability and provides encouragement for spiritual growth. Jesus is calling disciples,
not institutional members.

Our children pursue membership through this
same process. A Vital Christianity class is offered for
high school students. They do not go through a traditional confirmation experience prior to this time.
Maturity and the understanding of covenant are
important.

My daughter, Kristen, a freshman in high school,
just affirmed the covenant of membership at Ginghamsburg this past year. Prior to this "confirmation"
experience she had participated in the building of
two homes in Appalachia, worked on an inner-city
project in Chicago, spent a week with a mission team
in Jamaica, and worked on an inner-city children's
tutoring project for two years in Dayton. She has also
participated in a discipleship group for the last three
years. We want our youth to have a sense of the servant lifestyle of followers of Jesus before they affirm
a lifelong commitment to his church. Why rush people to the altar?

Each person is interviewed by a leadership team
before affirming the covenant of membership. Questions are asked concerning their faith journey, the
lordship of Christ, giftedness, service, small group
participation and stewardship.

Attendance is tracked. People are contacted by
letter or phone when they miss three weeks of worship. The membership roster is reviewed annually. An
inactive member is contacted and asked about his or
her intent to continue the covenant of membership at

Ginghamsburg. They are encouraged to become active in their journey. If they cannot do this they are asked to assume a relationship of "friend" to the congregation until they can again actively reaffirm the covenant of functioning member.

What Would John Wesley Say?

John Wesley's commitment to the covenant principle was crucial to the birth and vitality of the Methodist movement. Preaching and sacrament were not enough to renew old institutional bureaucracies and transform broken lives. People who were moved to commitment through anointed preaching tended to fall back into their old ways.

Wesley's genius lay in his ability to organize seekers and converts into vital discipleship groups called societies, classes and bands. Each step represented a systematic, progressive step in spiritual maturity. If you were to be a member in the Methodist movement you were expected to participate in a weekly group called a society. As the societies grew they were subdivided into small groups of 10 to 12 people. These groups were called class meetings and bands. Each class had a leader who was responsible for the spiritual development of the members and for collecting money for the poor. Those who were unwilling to be committed to the cell group were discontinued from membership in the society. Tickets were given to those who were faithful to the process. Without a ticket the member could not participate in the quarterly communion and love feast. If the member was not committed to the cell group during the second three-month period, his or her name was removed from membership in the Methodist society. Participation was not optional—it was expected.

The discipleship-accountability factor that Wesley's cell structure offered was the difference between

those converts who continued to grow in their faith
and commitment to Christ's mission and those who
fell back into their old complacent ways (See Appendix B, Rules of the Band).

We have found that people can quickly find their
way out the back door of the church if they don't
become established in a small group after the process
of membership. People stay in a church because they
find fulfillment through significant relationships
and responsibilities. Relationships are not formed in a
crowd! The people who thrive in the ministry at
Ginghamsburg are those who have made intimate
friendships in HOME (Homes Open for Ministry and
Encouragement) groups. These cell groups also provide a sense of healthy peer pressure that reinforces
growth and transformation in the new disciple.

Wesley understood that a church would be only
as strong as its members. Institutional club members
breed institutionalism. Transformed body members
transform whole communities and cultures.

The Life of the Body is in the Cell

Criticism and accusations did not stop Wesley's
approach to covenant membership. Persons who
wanted to join the Methodist movement needed first
to spend three months in a cell, where a well-trained,
mature leader taught the basics of the faith and discipleship. They could then be recommended for
membership, but only on the condition that they
were willing to submit themselves to the ongoing
accountability and discipline of the cell. Their con-
tinual involvement was evaluated quarterly. Each
week the members challenged each other's progress
in relationship to spiritual maturity and involvement
with the poor.

Wesley insisted that his people not divorce personal piety from social action. Many of his followers

worked in soup kitchens, organized meals-on-wheels type programs and distributed clothing and medicine to the poor. Wesley understood that the best way to get close to God was not by our religious acts but our actions toward people. Your behavior with people, especially poor and disenfranchised people, gives you power with God (see Isaiah 58; Micah 6:6; John 13:35). Jesus said, "just as you did it to one of the least of these who are members of my family, you did it to me" (Matthew 25:40). The test of authentic discipleship is what we are doing to people. Your actions and attitudes toward people are your actions and attitudes toward God.

> "... for I was hungry and you gave me food, I was thirsty and you gave me something to drink, I was a stranger and you welcomed me, I was naked and you gave me clothing, I was sick and you took care of me, I was in prison and you visited me" (Matthew 25:35–36).

Balanced discipleship happens in the ongoing, nurturing environment of accountability that the cell group provides. Discipleship and discipline are one and the same. Robert Chiles writes,

> On many occasions, Wesley observed that the decline and deadness of a society was the result of disregard for discipline. He laments, "I met the classes; but found no increase in the society. No wonder, for discipline has been quite neglected; and without this, little good can be done among the Methodists."[1]

For the purpose of vitality and accountability, membership progress was reviewed regularly. Covenant membership was not taken lightly in the early Methodist movement. There was no concept of life-long institutional membership. Ongoing membership was based on accountability, discipline, progressive

maturity and involvement with the poor. Membership was reviewed and renewed quarterly.

People will generally give according to the level
of expectation. Groups that expect more from people
tend to get more. This can be seen in groups like the
Mormons where many of their young people give at
least one year to full-time missionary service.

Covenant membership heightens expectation and
commitment. Last year the 800 members of Ginghamsburg church gave more than 1.6 million dollars
toward our mission. Men and women will leave work
early to drive a van load of teenagers to one of our
"Clubhouse" ministries to work with children after
school. Many more will spend much of their vacation
serving Christ's purpose of reaching the lost and
setting the oppressed free. Elevating the standards for
membership elevates expectation and the quality of
participation.

What is a Body Life Member?

A body life member is committed to Jesus Christ
as Savior and Lord. Savior. That is the good news!
Grace. The undeserved favor of God!

I was raised in the church but I didn't understand
until I was almost 20 years old that we don't earn
God's favor by trying to be good people. We could
never be good enough to meet God's standard. God
has done for us in Jesus Christ what we could never do
for ourselves. He has made it possible for us to know
that all our past, present and future sins are forgiven.
We can be certain that we will spend eternity in his
presence. Christ shows us that nothing can separate us
from God's love, not even our worst failures!

Our performance-oriented, co-dependent culture
needs to hear the good news of God's undeserved
favor that can be discovered in his Son, Jesus Christ.
Many of us who name Jesus as our Savior continue to

jump through hoops of performance to earn the favor
of God and others. This results in fragile self-esteem
and unhealthful, co-dependent relationships. God's
salvation in Christ is the truth that will bring health
to our relationship with God, our attitudes about
ourselves, and relationships with others.

Jesus Christ does not just save us for heaven. He
saves us to be fully human today. I was being interviewed by a reporter from the Dayton *Daily News*
about the rapid growth of Ginghamsburg church. He
asked me, "How do you keep your ego from running
away from you?" I replied, "That's easy. I know what I
have the potential to become." The temptations that
invade my thought life with varying degrees of intensity show my potential to have the morality of my
schnauzer. I need a Savior who saves me from my
darkest possibilities and allows me to have the integrity to be a faithful husband and father today.

I enjoy nice things. Nice suits, expensive ties,
designer jeans and classic cars clamor for my energies.
Forty thousand people die every day on this planet
for the lack of food. Forty thousand people a day and
I am thinking about *things!* I need a Savior today to
save me from my selfishness and to turn me outward
to be a servant to others. I need a Savior to save me
from the golden calf of consumerism.

To be a member of Christ's body means that you
recognize him as Lord. "Lord" means absolute author-
ity-owner. Periodically I teach a course at a local
seminary. I had been talking about the concept of
slave as it related to the lordship of Jesus Christ. Vol-
unteerism is the language of the club. Slave is the
language of the kingdom of God. One of the women
came up to me just before class and boldly asserted, "If
you use that word 'slave' one more time I am going to
get up and walk out. Slave has a negative connotation
in our culture today." I was taken aback. Her comment
really bothered me. But after some reflection it oc-

curred to me that the word "slave" has always had a
negative connotation. It has not been a popular occu-
pation in any culture. A slave is not something that
anyone ever wanted to be, but it is the only word that
lets me know that I am no longer in charge of my
own destiny.

Martin Luther said that the first words out of a
Christian's mouth when they get out of bed in the
morning should be "I am baptized." "Baptized" means
dead, buried and out of the way so that God can in-
habit my body and do with me as he pleases. It is like
the *Invasion of the Body Snatchers.* It looks like me
and sounds like me but it is really only my body,
invaded by the Holy Spirit, perpetrating the reality of
God's kingdom. God has access to all of my possessions, bank accounts and relationships. "Baptized"
means dead to my agendas, prejudices and percep-
tions and alive to the will and actions of Christ.

Too many of us bring our own agendas and prejudices to the places where decisions are made in our
churches. Our decisions reflect the values of our
culture more than the kingdom of God. We vote our
Republican or Democrat agendas, our liberal or conservative persuasions. We must empty ourselves of
everything so that we can truly reflect the mind of
Christ. Only then will the world look at the church
and see a movement that mirrors the kingdom of God
and not the prevailing culture.

A story is told about a group of Mennonites in
Vietnam during the Vietnam war. Mennonites are
pacifists and they had been ministering in the country for years trying to win the Vietnamese to Jesus.
When the war broke out they continued their efforts,
providing food and medical supplies to persons in
both North and South Vietnam.

The American government attempted to have
them move out of North Vietnam, stating that for an
American citizen to aid the enemy during war time is

equivalent to being a traitor to the United States. The Mennonite reply was significant: "We are citizens of the kingdom of God and our allegiance is to our King. Our King says, 'When your enemy hungers, feed them.'" When we accept Jesus Christ as our Lord and Savior, our allegiance to him is higher than to anyone else. Jesus Christ must be the supreme authority in our lives.

Do you accept Jesus Christ as your Lord and Savior and pledge your allegiance to his kingdom? That means you can have no higher allegiances in your life. Your allegiance to Christ and his kingdom must supersede your allegiance to country, family or vocation. To follow Jesus and enter into a covenant relationship with his body means that he is your highest authority.

A Body Life Member is Connected to Christ's People

One of the tragic heresies in the church today is the individualistic attitude that it can be just me and Jesus. Me and Jesus and the TV.

The church as the body of Christ is a living organism, not an organization. I cannot be connected to the Head if I am disconnected from the body, and I cannot be connected to the body if I am disconnected from the Head. Juan Carlos Ortiz reminds us that our elbows are members of our bodies because they are connected and functioning. The elbow receives instruction from the head and passes instruction on. It receives nourishment and passes nourishment on. It is not a member because its name is on a body members' list.

A covenant member accepts all of the responsibilities and liabilities that go with Christ's mission. If you are not receiving instruction from the Head and passing instruction on you are not a body member. If

you are not receiving nourishment and passing nourishment on you are not functioning as a member of
the body of Christ.

When I accepted Jesus as Lord of my life I was
born into his body, the church. You cannot commit
your life to Jesus and not become an active part of the
body. The church is the living presence of Christ in
the world. To be committed to Christ is to be connected and functioning with his people. A covenant
member must no longer make excuses for not sup-
porting Christ's mission with money, time, prayer and
service. A covenant member must be dead, buried and
free from the priorities and goals of the world. Christ
must have full access to all that they are and all that
they have. They must be fully committed to his purpose of reaching the lost and setting the oppressed
free.

As members of the body of Christ we are the only
hands, feet, mouthpiece and bank account that Jesus
has on this earth. Membership is that place in one's
spiritual pilgrimage where you say "I do" to this responsibility. The sacrament of baptism is not enough
to define the role of membership. You cannot carry
someone to commitment. Each person must give his
or her own response to the command "Follow me."

It costs something to be a follower of Jesus Christ.
In times of renewal the church rediscovers this important principle. The integrity of membership cannot
be divorced from the cost of discipleship. Jesus is
calling disciples, not club members.

Notes

1 Robert E. Chiles, *Scriptural Christianity: A Call to John
    Wesley's Disciples.* Francis Asbury Press, Zondervan
    Corporation, Grand Rapids, Michigan, 1984, 75.

The Priesthood PRINCIPLE

**Equipping the
Laity for Ministry**

Chapter Five

*Churches need to be allowing their lay people to be
in ministry. They need to be stretching them. They need
to be teaching them. They need to be challenging them.
They need to give them that chance to fail. . . . I'm so
thankful for the chance that I had. It changed my life.*

> *Sharon Amos, Member at
> Ginghamsburg Church*

The Business of the Church

So much of our energy in the church is spent in
meetings where we plan dinners and bazaars and
discuss such critical issues as what color to paint the
fellowship hall. What really is the business of the
church?

The apostle Paul, in the fourth chapter of Ephesians, tells us that Christ gave some to be apostles,
some to be prophets, some to be evangelists, and some
to be pastors and teachers, for the purpose of preparing God's people for the work of ministry. This is the
primary business of the church; to enable our people
to know Jesus as Lord and then to equip them for
ministry.

The New Testament church did not have seminaries for the privileged few to attend, learn to become
professionals, and then return to minister to specta-

tors. Many of our people sitting in committees are not "doing" ministry. At best they are only approving ministry for the professionals to carry out.

I recently talked to a young family man who had left his county-seat church to come to Ginghamsburg church. "I have grown tired of sitting in meetings that have nothing to do with the kingdom of God," he told me with a sense of resolve. "I have spent the last year and a half of my life on a worship committee that has done nothing more than bicker about replating the cross above the altar. One faction wants to redo it in brass, citing cost and durability as the consideration. The other half of the group wants it plated in gold."

Haven't most of us served on a committee like this at one time or another? This project could have been entrusted to one wise person in the congregation who could have gotten the job done quickly without wasting others' valuable frontline mission time.

The New Testament church functioned as a seminary that raised up the laity from the inside and then turned them loose on the outside. When Paul went to establish a new church, he evangelized, established the new believers in the faith, equipped them for ministry and then moved on to repeat this process in another place. When he left, a bishop didn't reappoint a new pastor from another church, nor did the church form a pastoral search committee. The pastors came out of the local church body. The church functioned as a seminary, equipping its own people for the purpose of frontline mission.

The church in renewal rediscovers this important New Testament principle—the priesthood of all believers. There is no special caste system under the new covenant like the Levitical priesthood in the old. All who name Jesus as Lord are priests. We are all called to be co-laborers in his mission in the world. This principle lies at the heart of every renewal movement throughout the history of the church. Releasing the laity for ministry in the world is the key to the success of Christ's mission.

In the eighth chapter of Acts we read that the church experienced the first great persecution.

> That day a severe persecution began against the church in Jerusalem, and all except the apostles were scattered throughout the countryside of Judea and Samaria (Acts 8:1).

The apostles were the professional pastors. We read later in that passage:

> Now those who were scattered went from place to place, proclaiming the word (v. 4).

What was the secret behind the early church's success in spreading the gospel to the uttermost parts of the earth? The laity had been equipped to be ministers and to proclaim the word, so the professionals remained in Jerusalem where they continued to equip others to do ministry in Jesus' name. The gospel was spread by the lay people!

This principle was at the heart of the Protestant Reformation. Luther reaffirmed this new covenant strategy that there is but one high priest, Jesus, and we are all priests ministering in the same body under his authority.

We need to be careful in labeling the different ministry functions in the church. Our labeling systems tend to separate clergy from the laity. At Ginghamsburg church we don't make the distinction of separating our professional clergy from the laity with the title "minister." We are all ministers. I don't say that I am a minister and you are a layperson. I am a pastor. A pastor is a function in the body, not a position. A pastor has a function in the same sense that a teacher, or a person with the gift of administration or the gift of helping has an equally important function.

There is only one position that is defined in the body
and that position is Jesus Christ, the head.

The Distinction Becomes Blurred

Once we start trying to say, "This is your
sphere, clergy," and "this is your sphere, laity,"
for me, it is always a sign of . . . a dying church.
A church that has the time to try and do those
rigid definitions is a church collapsing into itself. If you are out there spreading the gospel
of Christ and infiltrating the culture with that
gospel, you don't have time to make those
kind of definitions. You are out there working, arm in arm, hand in hand. There is a renewed sense of the priesthood of all believers,
and that is absolutely vital and essential for
the renewed church.

Dr. Leonard Sweet

Someone recently asked me, "Who are the professional pastors around here anyway?" When the
church is at its best you can't tell the professionals
from the rest of the players.

John Wesley capitalized on this principle when
he sent out "lay" circuit riders throughout the British
Isles and then all across the continent of America.
Most Methodist churches saw the circuit rider only
once a quarter. The circuit rider would serve the
sacraments and take care of weddings. The lay people
carried on the business of worship, teaching, evangelism and social ministries 12 out of 13 weeks. They
continued with worship, Sunday school and mission
work in the weeks that the professional pastor was
not there.

The Baptist and Methodist movements saw incredible growth during the Second Great Awakening.
One of the reasons you see a United Methodist church
and Baptist church in almost every county in the

United States today is due to their dependence upon the laity. The Methodist movement spread westward through the circuit rider, who lacked formal training by professional, ecclesiastical standards. The Baptists grew through the farmer who farmed by day and functioned as lay pastor by night.

Those churches that made a clear distinction between the professional clergy and the laity and emphasized a high standard of educational training for the clergy remained in the East for the most part. Not much happened in the Episcopal and Congregational churches during the Second Great Awakening because of their focus on "professional" ministry.

Organic Ministry

Look at the way that God has spread his gifts throughout the church.

> To each is given the manifestation of the Spirit for the common good. To one is given through the Spirit the utterance of wisdom, and to another the utterance of knowledge according to the same Spirit, to another faith by the same Spirit, to another gifts of healing by the one Spirit, to another the working of miracles, to another prophecy, to another the discernment of spirits, to another various kinds of tongues, to another the interpretation of tongues. All these are activated by one and the same Spirit, who allots to each one individually just as the Spirit chooses.... Indeed, the body does not consist of one member but of many (1 Corinthians 12:7-11, 14).

There are no superstars in the body of Christ. Not one of us has all of the gifts. I am limited in what I can do in ministry. God has gifted me to lead and to teach biblical truth in relevant ways, but I don't have other "pastoral" gifts that many would expect the "professional minister" to have. Many expect the professional pastor to function as a personal chaplain who is hired to do everything. This professional model of ministry is not biblical.

We are meant to function in interdependent relationships with each other as the Spirit works through us. This is an organic model of ministry. Each of us has a different function in the body. One function is not more important than another. We have been baptized by the same Spirit and are all part of the same body. But there are "varieties of gifts" and "varieties of services" and "varieties of activities."

When the bishop laid his hands upon me and ordained me to the ministry of word, sacrament and order, ordination did not give me more of the Spirit, an elevated calling over the "non-ordained," or really anything that God had not already given me or called me to do.

God has set each of us apart and consecrated us for his purpose in the body of Christ. For the body to function according to God's purpose each member must be encouraged to function as God's priest. The church must intentionally help people identify God's call. Equipping the saints for the work of ministry—this is the business of the church!

I would like to introduce you to someone from Ginghamsburg church who demonstrates this principle.

The Chicken Parts Expert

I first met Sharon Amos when her daughter, Kim, began coming to the youth group during her freshman year in high school. We were planning a summer mission trip and I had a meeting with parents to explain the purpose of the trip and to share my expectations. After this meeting Sharon told me that she was going to be married in a few weeks and move south of the Dayton area. Kim would not be able to participate in the youth program because of the distance.

The first Sunday morning after the wedding Kim got up at 6:30 a.m. and went to her mom and new stepdad's bedroom.

"Mom, wake up! Will you give me a ride to the Dayton Mall where I can catch a bus to Vandalia, and then get a ride with one of my friends to Ginghamsburg church?"

Sharon could not believe what she was hearing, but she got up, drove her daughter to the Dayton Mall, where Kim caught a bus and rode 28 miles to Vandalia, Ohio, and then met a friend who drove her the remaining five miles to the church.

The next Sunday morning the same scenario unfolded at 6:30 a.m.

"Mom–Wayne. Will one of you take me to the mall so I can catch the bus to Vandalia and then get a ride to the church?"

Sharon assured herself that this would be a three- or four-week fad at most, but Kim's Sunday morning ritual continued for three months. The Amoses finally decided to get up and bring Kim themselves to see what kind of "organization" this was that had such a grip on their daughter.

They came out of curiosity, but soon became convinced that the message of Jesus they heard at Ginghamsburg church was not only worth the drive but the way of life. Sharon and Wayne grew to understand that belief equals commitment, which equals service. Both of them began using their gifts and talents in serving Christ's mission. They started out by traveling with the teens on mission work projects. They worked in Mexico, Chicago, New York City and Pittsburgh. Half of their vacation time was committed to mission trips.

Sharon began teaching Sunday school, leading discipleship groups, and going on every possible youth trip. She also had the responsibility of a full-time professional job. She was a chicken-parts expert. I am not exactly sure what this involved, but it was related to the food brokerage industry and restaurant sales. Sharon eventually dropped down to part-time status in her professional job in order to donate 20 hours per week to our youth ministry team.

God had given Sharon a vision. She had seen God's burning bush. After working with Habitat for Humanity and other building projects in various cities, Sharon and Wayne began the Dayton work project, a ministry involving insulating, painting and rehabilitating housing for low-income families. They rented a dorm at Wright State University and held work camps for youth who would come for a week at a time and grow in their faith in Jesus while serving others. The project ran for five weeks that first summer.

At the end of the five-week period I began to get phone calls from other churches around the state asking if Sharon Amos could come and be their youth minister. Sharon had never been to seminary! She was a chicken-parts expert! Sharon moved on from Ginghamsburg church and became the youth minister at a church in West Carrollton.

The church must function as a seminary that equips the laity for the mission of Christ.

Developing the Curriculum

A seminary has a curriculum. If the local church is going to be a seminary that equips laity for ministry, then we need to be serious about developing a curriculum that will give lay ministers the necessary skills and knowledge for mission.

Our whole strategy of ministry at Ginghamsburg is focused on this ministry of equipping. (This strategy is discussed further under the Leadership Principle in the next chapter). We have built our curriculum through the following areas:

Vital Christianity. This is our 13-week membership class that focuses on basic Christianity. The first third of the class deals with the person of Jesus Christ, his claims, his purpose and his authority. The rest of the course deals with the Holy Spirit, spiritual gifts, Christian growth and the meaning of covenant membership. Commitment to the Lordship of Jesus Christ, the ability to articulate the gospel clearly, a servant lifestyle and visible commitment to the local church are essential entry points for the person who will serve in ministry. (See Appendix A: Vital Christianity Course Outline.)

Sunday school. Most of our classes are electives that change every quarter. At least one third of these classes are designed for the purpose of equipping people for particular ministries. There are classes for youth counselors, Sunday school teachers, small-group leaders and various other ministries. Sunday school teachers take a training class during a quarter when they are not teaching.

Special training events. An example of this would be the weekend retreat for all people in teaching ministries. We bring in education specialists in the areas of preschool, elementary, youth and adult ministries. We also sponsor an annual leadership retreat for all of the leaders in the church. This is an important time for me to share my continued vision for the mission of Ginghamsburg church with those who are so essential to its success.

Ministry area. Each of the ministry areas in our church has a particular strategy for discipleship. The Stephen ministers (lay care and counselling) go through a two-year weekly training process. At the end of that time they are consecrated for ministry.

Weekend conferences. These conferences cover such topics as healing, ministry to persons with AIDS and their families, cell-group ministry, divorce recovery, renewal and singles ministries.

Trinity Bible series. This is a ten-semester Bible survey course designed to help Christians become biblically literate. We encourage all of our people to take at least the first two semesters, Old and New Testament survey. Many other resources are available such as the Bethel Bible Series and the United Methodist Discipleship Bible study series.

On-the-job training. There is no better way to learn than by the hands-on experience of doing. Our people are first tested as workers before they are given the responsibility of leadership. This takes place through a mentoring process. A person first works as an assistant teacher, or an apprentice cell-group leader, or begins to help at youth functions on Sunday evenings or on mission trips. This approach allows people to grow into ministry and gives leadership ample time for observation.

Sending laity to key training events. Most pastors are given money for continuing education. If pastoral ministry and lay ministry are equal, then we must budget money for lay continuing education. We send a group of youth counselors every year to the youth specialties national convention. We have sent laity to Fuller Institute training events in California. If it is the business of the church to equip laity for the purpose of ministry, then we must invest in the education of the laity.

Accountability

If our commitment to the priesthood principle is going to have vital consequences, one area that we cannot overlook is accountability. People who accept the high calling of Christ must be equally willing to accept his high standard. We cannot approach ministry with the idea that "I am a volunteer and you should be thankful for anything that I am willing to give." Christ does not call volunteers. He calls servants. These servants are people who are actively hearing God's call and following Jesus in the way of the Cross. By the very act of following Christ they have committed themselves to his standard of social and moral integrity. They are fully invested with their time and resources in Christ's mission of winning the lost and setting the oppressed free.

The people we recruit for ministry need to understand this standard up front. It is better to let a position go unfilled than to recruit a lukewarm person to fill it. Our ministry standard and expectation is clearly explained before a person begins his or her ministry (see Appendix C, the Teacher's Covenant). The Teacher's Covenant is presented to all teachers at Ginghamsburg church before they begin their teaching ministry. It indicates our expectations, our commitment and the accountability factor that we maintain.

But I'm Just an Ordinary Person . . .

As you have been reading along, have any of these thoughts crossed your mind?

> Ginghamsburg church has really gotten its act together and everything is working well there. The professional ministers place trust in the laity. They practice the priesthood of all believers and the layperson is encouraged and supported in ministry. Ginghamsburg church utilizes a curriculum for strengthening lay ministry and an accountability structure is in place. They have exceptional lay persons like Sharon Amos, a person with vision, who

knows her function in the body, and has the knowledge and enthusiasm to do something with it. That's great for Ginghamsburg church, but it would never work in my church. I go to an ordinary church and I'm just an ordinary person ...

Frequently I get feedback from visiting laypersons that involves a mixture of hope and perplexity. A typical visitor to Ginghamsburg church might say something like this:

I am fascinated and in awe of the tremendous variety of ministry that is occurring at Ginghamsburg church. I wish we could do that in my church, but we simply don't have that kind of leadership, and we laypersons don't know how or where to begin on our own.

Visitors get excited because they like what they find at Ginghamsburg and they want to carry their excitement back to their own church. Laity want to be involved in meaningful ministry. Their questions impress me with their earnest desire to serve Christ more completely, which is hidden behind more direct questions like: "Mike, how do I get started in my own church? How do I know that God is speaking to me? What could I do to bring this kind of new life into my congregation?"

Pastors visiting Ginghamsburg have similar questions and comments.

Mike, what I see happening at Ginghamsburg church is my dream for my congregation. I am fascinated and in awe of the tremendous variety of ministry that is occurring at Ginghamsburg church. I want to see my lay people more involved and on fire for Christ. I wish our church could develop new ministries like Ginghamsburg church has, but we simply don't have that kind of congregation. My members expect me to do the pastoral planning and ministry... it's just a different kind of place. This would never work in my congregation.

I began to wonder about these comments and asked a few questions of my own: "Does Ginghamsburg have exceptional people or is our ministry carried on by ordinary people? Is Ginghamsburg really so different? How did all these extensive ministries get started?"

At Ginghamsburg church, youth ministry is involved in day-to-day local mission outreach, week-long mission trips, youth leadership training, youth praise teams, leading congregational worship several times a year and producing a top-notch drama production each year. Where did all this begin? How did Mike Nygren know that God wanted him to do youth ministry? Do the people who are leading successful ministry areas at Ginghamsburg have some type of unique spirituality about them? Or are they just ordinary people? My mind began churning over these questions and I felt compelled to seek answers.

The business of the church is to know Jesus and to make him known to others. I know how professional pastors do this, but how does a layperson know that he or she is called to do a specific task? How do they find their unique calls of Jesus and get started in ministry? Does God really speak to individuals, ordinary people, today? How do "ordinary people" hear God's direction? "There is only one thing to do," I thought to myself, "ask the experts."

Where Do I Find My Burning Bush?

It was not difficult mentally to identify some "burning bush experts" at Ginghamsburg. Looking at the existing ministry areas and recalling the people

instrumental in the beginnings of each ministry, I
came up with a few questions to ask—questions that
other people ask me. My respondents are ordinary
people. They have not gone to seminary. None has
taken a course in "How to Begin a New Ministry." They
were not given a list of things to do to begin a Clubhouse, Kids' Camp or a Women's ministry. They are
vastly different in personality and religious background, and they have profoundly different ideas
about how to accomplish their goals. Their common
denominator is that they felt a need to pursue a certain ministry. They saw a burning bush. They had a
vision for a particular ministry, to meet a particular
need. God spoke to them in some manner, communi-
cating to each of them his plans, dreams and visions.
They all have a passion to serve Jesus as he has shown
them how and where to serve. And they have all
heard a different call at Ginghamsburg.

Mike, our youth director, had this to share concerning his entrance into youth ministry and God's
call upon his life for this ministry:

> If I was "called," there was no burning bush, no
> visible and outright affirmation to give up my
> painting business to pursue youth ministry,
> but rather I had this inner passion that recog-
> nized how God could use me in the lives of
> teens.

Carolyn's reply was similar. She listened to a verse
that haunted her. She responded. And the early stages
of women's ministry came into existence.

> My vision for an active women's ministry
> originated on a walk around my neighbor-
> hood. Luke describes Jesus' challenge to enter
> into the harvesting process and his plea for us
> to join in as laborers in his harvest. That verse
> kept haunting me as I walked past the houses
> surrounding my own home.

Carolyn also spoke of our unique ministries, and the plans that God has for each of us. She went on to give instructions on hearing, responding to and defining our unique roles:

> I believe that God creates each of us individually and uniquely, and deep within our makeup are the seeds of the ministry he has prepared for us. If we believe Psalm 139:13-16 and Jeremiah 1:4-5 and 29:11, then we know that God has plans for us! Living a life of yieldedness and obedience, and listening for the voice of the Spirit, allows God to work those plans through us. I believe he matches us up according to temperaments, natural talents, interests and spiritual gifts with the plan he has for us. In other words, he equips us to follow his call—even before we are born!

What actions did Carolyn take in the early stages of the present Women's Ministry?

> I began a neighborhood Bible study for women, which grew from nine to 30. Then we moved into the church, divided into several groups, and had 75-100 women involved in what became Morning With a Purpose. From this beginning we have grown to a ministry impacting over 400 women through a variety of ministries: retreats, Evening With a Purpose, Morning With a Purpose, Christian aerobics, a mentoring ministry, outreach to inner-city moms and a planned outreach to preschool moms. The key has been to allow other women to see their own burning bushes—the place where they hear the voice of God calling them. Also significant is fostering their natural bent to ministry (interests, talents and personalities), developing their spiritual gifts and deepening their walk with Christ. The

bottom line is putting it all under the rule and authority of Christ.

I asked Lou Walthall to relate the earliest memories of children's ministry at Ginghamsburg. Under Lou's leadership ministry to children expanded and flourished, and new avenues of ministering to children were developed.

Since the early 1970s I had dreamed of having my own preschool but I never thought I'd have the opportunity for this dream to come true. I remember sharing this dream with Mike Slaughter and he challenged me not to have "my" preschool but to move toward a preschool that belonged to Jesus and was committed to making him the focus. It sounded good, but as I looked at the old church building I knew that there was no way! Without the right facility the dream was impossible. How wrong could I be?

Ginghamsburg church seemed to be on the cutting edge in so many areas but no one had a vision for helping children find Christ in a personal way and for providing experiences so they could grow in their relationship with him. I began to ask questions and make my concerns known. I could not have verbalized it at the time but God was giving me that vision.

When I became children's ministry coordinator I began looking at the needs of each age level and began developing ministries to meet those needs. Sitting at the kitchen table one day, I realized that this is different. This was no longer "doing my duty" for the church. This was God's plan for ministry! I had no idea how big God's plan, his vision, could and would be! In 1984 we moved into the new discipleship center and Ginghamsburg Preschool opened its doors. We were thrilled with our 19 students. The school has served well over 600 students since 1984.

Mike Nygren had words of wisdom and stories about different areas of teen ministry and its development at Ginghamsburg. He spoke of how the teen mission plans developed, where the vision comes and our ability to dream God's dream:

> Missions is a maturing process. We should start in our own backyard, making sure we really understand who we are as individuals, as a church, and as a community. We need to see what we are doing from the perspective of Jesus, and also to see what else needs to be done.
>
> To dream we must simply be open to listen to God. To accomplish the dreams we must be willing to go where God leads us, even if it is new or alien to us.
>
> For churches to develop an outward journey strategy they need to be willing to think beyond what they already do or are comfortable with.... Outward journey ministry focuses on seeing the world's needs through the eyes of Jesus, and then working toward meeting those needs. The transforming part of our journeys has come through patience and perseverance and by being attentive to the opportunities around us.

Mike spoke of the early Clubhouse ministries:

> Our youth group is currently involved in an after-school ministry in the inner city of Dayton. For 112 of the 180 school days of the year our teens show up for this ministry to 15-20 children. It's not easy to coordinate this min-

istry, but it works. I believe youth ministry has the opportunity of teaching values of life we all need to have. This after-school ministry came about after two years of involvement one day a week with these children. It progressed to two days a week the following year, and finally now to four. The teens were encouraged to dream, and the dream turned into a reality. The reality today is a rented storefront we renovated and now call "The Clubhouse."

Another annual event, the Thanksgiving Dinner, regularly serves 400 people in need. The entire meal is planned and prepared by teens, as Mike explains:

I thought of the Norman Rockwell image of Thanksgiving dinner, with a festive family around a table overflowing with not only food, but with love. So, the dream was born to provide a dinner to our small community that would fill both of these needs, which seem to arise especially on Thanksgiving Day. We would be the families that many in the community were missing on Thanksgiving Day. Why do we keep doing the dinner, year after year? I suspect that [our guests find] the holiday with us just a little more enjoyable, a little less lonely. Likewise, the teens could have stayed home all day. but I suspect that their lives also would have been a little emptier. That is why we have the dinner every year, year after year.

One of our teens, Robin Gale, was featured in an article in a local newspaper. Robin was then a 17-year-old high school senior and a paid intern at the Clubhouse. She directed more than 30 teen volunteers in ministering to the local children in the after-school program. She also had served in Jamaica, Mexico, New

York and in other local projects. Robin states, "I'm the kind of person who needs to be doing something. It scares me to think what I'd be if I hadn't become a Christian and found a place to plug myself in."

Richard, a youth counselor who works with Mike Nygren, said this about the beginnings of Dream Builders, a ministry that restores dilapidated houses in the inner city:

> I think the idea for a new ministry comes from within the body, the church, as an outgrowth of something that is already happening. I see it as a group process, taking some involvement, improving upon it, and dreaming together. The vision was already planted in me for DreamBuilders, but I needed other believers to help me see the vision, to identify the voids and to find the opportunities to plug in to fill these gaps in our ministry.

This panel of experts answered some of my other questions as well.

How do ordinary people dream God's dream?

1. Read God's Word.
2. Hang around God's people.
3. Listen for God to speak through his people.
4. Listen for his voice.
5. Open yourself—say, "Here I am, Lord, send me."
6. Don't wait for the perfect time, perfect people and perfect ministry before serving. Get in there and serve and God will show you his dream.

—Lou

Where do I find ministry opportunities?

> I know this sounds funny, but they need to open their eyes. Too often we look for a bolt of lightening or writing across the sky when we really need

to open our eyes and look at the needs around us.
As we see the needs I believe they become our
burning bush.

—Lou

How do you take an idea deep within you and turn it into a reality?

First, I would encourage people to share their
dream with someone they trust. Next, be patient
and allow the dream to percolate and watch for
doors to open. Open doors to me are usually
seeing a real need for the ministry, other Christians who say "go for it," other people who want
to be involved in the ministry, financial resources.
Next, I would say, don't be afraid to fail. If it is
God's plan he will make it succeed (Proverbs 16:3).

—Lou

What about failure?

Having the door slammed in your face is not
always bad. At times I fall into the trap of dreaming my own dreams, and not God's dreams. I have
grown. (and learned about) changing challenges
into positive experiences, so I knew nothing was
impossible as we ventured into our tutoring
program. The tutoring program started slowly. It
was from this small venture that we would later
build "The Clubhouse" ministry.

—Mike

The rhythm continues. God's initiative; my obedience. His plan within me; my response in action no
matter where the path may lead. God's plan for ministry; my call to fulfill that which is deep within me
and to be God's hands and feet in the world. We, lay
and clergy alike, are in ministry together, following
the agenda of Jesus to make him known and to lead
his people to wholeness. This is the business of the
church in renewal. (Appendix D provides a brief

listing of the variety of ministries initiated and con-
ducted at Ginghamsburg church).

It is the business of the church to help people
identify God's burning bushes. Then we must throw
gasoline, not water, on their burning bush. Visions
must be nurtured by leaders. We will explore this in
greater depth in the next chapter.

The Leadership
PRINCIPLE

Spiritual
Entrepreneurship

Chapter Six

Do not neglect the gift that is in you, which was given to you through prophecy with the laying on of hands by the council of elders. Put these things into practice, devote yourself to them, so that all may see your progress. Pay close attention to yourself and to your teaching; continue in these things, for in doing this you will save both yourself and your hearers (1 Timothy 4: 14-16).

The need was never so great. A chronic crisis of governance—that is, the pervasive incapacity of organizations to cope with the expectations of their constituents—is now an overwhelming factor worldwide. If there was ever a moment in history when a comprehensive strategic view of leadership was needed, not just by a few leaders in high office but by large numbers of leaders in every job, from the factory floor to the executive suite, from a McDonald's fast food franchise to a law firm, this is certainly it.[1]

Warren Bennis and Burt Nanus

Often I hear the question, "What will happen to this church if Mike leaves? So much of what has happened at Ginghamsburg church has been dependent on Mike's leadership." My answer is, "Who knows what will happen? It depends on whether I'm followed by effective, anointed leadership."

There is a tendency to downplay the importance of leadership in the institutional church and to invalidate models of success where a person is clearly identified as a catalyst. The system is confused by successful leaders. Who will replace them when they leave? Where do you send them? Leadership means change and the system resists change. As Jesus observed, institutions tend to stone their prophets.

Throughout church history there has been no example of renewal happening without a leader functioning as the catalyst. God has always used a human instrument as his agent for change. Abraham and Moses were the leaders associated with the old covenant and God's revelation through Judaism. God's promise of a unique people who would be priest to all nations was inspired through Abraham. The law that would mature and govern this people came through Moses.

Israel went through cycles of obedience, disobedience, repentance and renewal. God would use judges like Deborah, reforming kings like Hezekiah or Josiah, and prophets as his instruments for renewal.

Hezekiah was 25 years old when he became king.

> He did what was right in the eyes of the LORD, just as his father David had done. He removed the high places, smashed the sacred stones and cut down the Asherah poles. He broke into pieces the bronze snake Moses had made, for up to that time the Israelites had been burning incense to it. . . . Hezekiah trusted in the LORD, the God of Israel. There was no one like him. . . . He held fast to the LORD and did not cease to follow him; he kept the commands the LORD had given Moses (2 Kings 18:3-6).

These leaders would lead the people from dead institutional civil religion back into a vital covenant relationship with God. They inspired people to return to their first love.

Jesus and Paul are the leaders associated with God's revelation through the new covenant.

> "Do not think that I have come to abolish the Law or the Prophets; I have not come to abolish them but to fulfill them" (Matthew 5:17, NIV).

Jesus demonstrated the inner law of the renewed heart rather than rigid adherence to outward appearance through legalistic behavior. He was both the demonstration and fulfillment of loving God with all heart, soul and strength and loving one's neighbor as oneself.

Paul's energies launched this localized Jewish movement globally.

> For there is no difference between Jew and Gentile—the same Lord is Lord of all and richly blesses all who call on him, for, "Everyone who calls on the name of the Lord will be saved" (Romans 10:12, NIV).

Paul's missionary journeys and writings brought God's message of reconciliation through his son Jesus Christ to the "uttermost parts of the earth." It has impacted kings and kingdoms, calendar systems, politics and the arts, education and social programs. All because God chooses to act and speak through human instruments.

The church has also experienced repeated cycles of obedience and disobedience. God has raised up leaders throughout history who have acted as reformers in calling the church back to her first love. Augustine developed a systematic theology in the fourth century that helped give the church doctrinal stability in the midst of the rapidly growing cults. His work set a precedent for biblical integrity and trinitarian fidelity. His Christ-centered focus has influenced reformers' theology right up through the present time.

Luther was God's agent for renewal during the sixteenth century. The church had long since forgotten its first purpose. It had become a corrupt institutional bureaucracy that served the interest of the state rather than the purpose of God. Luther's posting of his Ninety-Five Theses on the door of the Castle Church in Wittenburg set in motion a revolution that cast off brittle wineskins. His bold leadership inspired new life and faith among the working-class people.

Ignatius Loyola, St. John of the Cross and Teresa of Avila were God's agents in leading the renewal movement in the Catholic Church, the Counter-Reformation,[2] during this same time period.

There has been a leader behind every awakening. John Calvin and his emphasis on the sovereignty of God and divine election further impacted Western Europe and the later Anabaptist movement. John Wesley's emphasis on individual responsibility and his disciplined approach to discipleship fueled the flames of renewal on two continents. Jonathan Edwards, Charles Finney, Billy Graham and Mother Teresa have all been agents of God's hand to further his kingdom's purpose.

All movements have been inspired by great leaders. Gandhi inspired the passive resistance movement that won India's freedom from Britain. Dr. Martin Luther King empowered the civil rights movement. Winston Churchill stepped forward and rallied his nation's courage in resisting and holding off Nazi Germany. Japan's incredible economic turnaround in quality control was inspired by the post-World War II business pioneer, W. Edwards Deming.

What should be obvious must be stated. We cannot go forward without effective leadership. We cannot solve present problems without effective leadership. Without effective leadership we cannot promote necessary change.

For the church the result is critically clear. Lack of leadership means decline and death. I have seen countless examples where a healthy church loses a healthy leader and then under new pastoral direction experiences significant decline in attendance and loss of focus. Not all leaders are equal and, even more significantly, most people in positions of leadership are not leaders! Leadership is not optional. The sheep need a shepherd.

A Critical Distinction

Leadership and management are not the same thing. Warren Bennis and Burt Nanus effectively clarify the difference.

> The problem with many organizations, and especially the ones that are failing, is that they tend to be overmanaged and underled. They may excel in the ability to handle the daily routine, yet never question whether the routine should be done at all. There is a profound difference between management and leadership, and both are important. "To manage" means "to bring about, to accomplish, to have charge of or responsibility for, to conduct." "Leading" is "influencing, guiding in direction, course, action, opinion." The distinction is crucial. Managers are people who do things right and leaders are people who do the right thing.[3]

The church is experiencing a major leadership crisis. We are skilled in the practice of century-old daily routines but lack the vision, knowledge and courage to do the right thing. We have many managers in the church but few leaders.

Leaders are Driven Forward by Vision

Leaders are the people who have seen burning bushes. They have heard God's voice. They have a very clear picture in their mind of what God wants them to accomplish. Vision enables the leader to discern God's direction. It gives clarity of purpose. The leader is able to articulate clearly the "why" and "where" and speaks with the authority of God.

One of the best biblical examples contrasting the difference between leadership and management can be seen in Moses and Aaron.

> Then Moses went up to God, and the LORD called to him from the mountain and said, "This is what you are to say to the house of Jacob and what you are to tell the people of Israel" ... So Moses went back and summoned the elders of the people and set before them all the words the Lord had commanded him to speak (Exodus 19:3, 7, NIV).

Moses' revelation of the vision to people leaves no sense that God's mandate is up for a vote.

The burning bush experience is not so clear for the manager. Aaron was not on the mountain with Moses to hear God speak. He was more pastoral in his relationship with people and more "hands on" in ministering to their needs. After all, Moses was never around when you really needed him. He would disappear for weeks at a time. He could have been accused of having his head up in the clouds, of being withdrawn and distant.

Aaron, on the other hand, was always there when you needed him. Many would consider him the ideal pastor. He didn't have the luxury of taking the time to climb a mountain and find a burning bush. The people's needs were too pressing.

Because the manager lacks a clear vision, he or she becomes more of a facilitator of group process. "What do you think we should do?" "How do you feel about it?" "Where do you think we should be headed?" The group facilitator role, however, fails to take into account one very critical problem. It is in the nature of people to want to go back to Egypt. It doesn't matter that Egypt represents slavery. Egypt is all we have ever known. Egypt represents the way that we have always done it in the past. There is no freedom or opportunity in Egypt but life there carries minimal risk and it is predictable. After all, none of us has ever seen this "promised land" that Moses keeps talking about. What little information we have tells us that there are insurmountable obstacles. Some among us speak of giants that can never be overcome on our meager resources.

If you put it up for a vote, you will go back to Egypt! Or you will bring Egypt to you by building a golden calf in the wilderness. With very good intentions, that is exactly what Aaron does. Through the facilitation of group process he enables the people to build a golden calf in God's name. He becomes the people's personal chaplain, managing their expectations by carrying on the sacred traditions that they have brought with them from Egypt. The manager does the expected thing. The leader is concerned with doing the right thing.

Never has this been more apparent to me than in the way we cling to outdated worship and music forms. I had just struggled through a highly liturgical, sparsely attended communion service. Even after six years of theological training I had trouble making heads or tails of the experience.

Afterwards, the pastor invited me for lunch. As we headed out of the parking lot onto a suburban street he apologized for the low attendance with the comment that "communion Sunday is always a low attendance week."

I could not help noticing the booming housing developments all around his church. Young families out in their yards, grilling, planting flowers, cutting grass and playing ball. At his urging, I commented, "You will never reach those families if you don't

change your worship style. Look at your own interest—you leave your radio set to an adult contemporary station."

He hesitated, loosened his tie, and then do you
know what he said?

"I know it won't work. But that is what these
people are used to. They have always done it this way.
They will have to make up their minds to change if
they want to grow."

I couldn't believe it! And I couldn't hold my
tongue. "These people are not going to decide to
change. They are in Egypt. Egypt is all they know.
That is why you have been sent here. You are here to
lead change. God has not sent you here to manage the
expected thing. He did not give his Son for the purpose of maintaining the status quo. He sent Jesus to
change it, and he has chosen you to be the leader."

A Leader's Dream is Shaped by Others

So Elijah went from there and found
Elisha son of Shaphat. He was plowing with
twelve yoke of oxen, and he himself was driv-
ing the twelfth pair. Elijah went up to him and
threw his cloak around him. Elisha then left
his oxen and ran after Elijah. "Let me kiss my
father and mother good-by," he said, "and then
I will come with you" (1 Kings 19:19-20, NIV).

God uses leaders to shape the dreams of leaders.
Dr. King's vision for the civil rights movement during
the 1950s and 1960s was greatly influenced by Ma-
hatma Gandhi's philosophy of leadership in the passive resistance movement in India. John Wesley adopted his strategy of discipleship through cell groups
from the Moravian leaders. George Whitefield influenced Wesley's method and style in field preaching.

Several "Bethlehem star" people and experiences
have helped shape and clarify my own vision.

Dietrich Bonhoeffer's *Cost of Discipleship* was one of the first books I read as a new Christian. From that point on I would always see and proclaim the cost of what it means to be a follower of Jesus Christ. Grace must never be seen as "cheap" nor sold like cut-rate wares at the market place.

My experience in Campus Crusade for Christ at the University of Cincinnati evoked in me a strong commitment to systematic discipleship. Our Vital Christianity program for new members was influenced by my Campus Crusade years.

Dr. Ken Kinghorn and his emphasis on the gifts of the Holy Spirit as the means to accomplish God's mission through the church has affected the approach I have taken in choosing my own involvement in ministry as well as involving others. We use a spiritual gifts-inventory to help people decide where to become actively involved in ministry at Ginghamsburg. My three years under Ken's influence during seminary forever shaped my understanding of empowerment for mission.

Tom Skinner was a radical influence in my life during the early 1970s. Through his ministry I saw the church as "God's new community on earth that modeled what was going on in heaven." The church is the community that "shows people what it is like when Jesus is in control." My commitment to blend a personal encounter with Jesus and social justice was shaped by my encounters with Tom Skinner.

Howard Snyder's books, *The Problem of Wineskins, The Radical Wesley,* and *The Community of the King* have shaped my thinking and approach to strategy and church structures. Developing "new wineskins to hold new wine" and the emphasis on moving people from meetings to front-line mission have evolved from his influence.

Don Joy, Mary Olson, Len Sweet and others have thrown gasoline on my burning bush along the way.

God uses Elijahs to shape the dreams of Elishas. Hanging out with the sold out enables one more clearly to dream God's dream.

> When the LORD was about to take Elijah up to heaven in a whirlwind, Elijah and Elisha were on their way from Gilgal. Elijah said to Elisha, "Stay here; the LORD has sent me to Bethel."
>
> But Elisha said, "As surely as the LORD lives and as you live, I will not leave you" (2 Kings 2:1-2, NIV).

Elisha knew that Elijah was a man who had heard God's voice. Whatever God had done for Elijah, or taught Elijah, Elisha wanted a double portion of it!

Seek out people of vision. Read whatever you can read. Ask questions. Go to seminars. During my early years at Ginghamsburg church I would travel to the Fuller Institute of Church Growth in Pasadena for seminars. We invited speakers like Juan Carlos Ortiz to come to our church. I would call effective pastors to see if I could catch a glimpse of what God was showing them. As I write this chapter I am preparing to go to Phoenix, Arizona, with my wife for a Leadership Network Conference. I have found that one of the best ways to see a burning bush is to find others who have seen one. Vision is contagious!

Leaders are Focused on Results

Leaders begin with the end in mind. They have a clear picture of what the destination looks like before they begin the journey.

When I came to Ginghamsburg church in April 1979 I was very concerned with finding out God's mission for the church. I knew that this little country church had been in existence since 1863. And I also knew that every one of the 90 people involved would have an opinion of his or her own. At 27 years of age I sensed that my life and ministry was too short to be about anything less than the purpose of God. So I established as my first priority to "see" God's purpose.

Throughout church history, leaders of renewal have been able to see beyond the immediate barriers of "culturefied tradition" to sense God's intent for purpose and direction.

On a chilly but sunny April morning I stood in a field behind the little two-room church building—the site of our current discipleship center. Staring back at the modest church facility that looked like hundreds of others, I said: "Lord, I am not going to leave this field until I have a clear sense of your mission for this church."

Vision and the fortitude to accomplish God's purpose grow out of our willingness to wade out across the stream and wrestle with God. We need a willingness to wrestle and not let go until we have a sense of resolve about God's direction: "God, show me. I will not let go or turn back if you assure me that you are with me."

We must first wrestle with God in our field of dreams if we are going to be able to speak to people with a sense of his authority. I prayed and I waited. For when we are sure that it is God's voice that we hear, we won't be so tempted to turn back in times of resistance.

I remained in the field for the rest of the afternoon. As is so often the case God speaks not through the storm, fire or earthquake but God comes through silence. His thoughts began to stream into my head. I could see 3000 people worshiping the Lord. A deep sense of God's heart for the lost overwhelmed me. I am not a highly emotional person, but tears ran down my cheeks as I sensed God's pain for the people who lived 30 minutes in every direction from this building who had no understanding of his love and healing intention. That intention had to be made known. The resurrected Christ has the power to break addictions, overcome co-dependent tendencies and restore broken relationships. He is not about condemnation but reconciliation.

I had a vision of a church that would be a teaching-equipping church. This would be a place where ordinary people would come and be equipped to be fully assimilated and functioning members of the body of Christ—disciples who would go out into the marketplace and win the lost, followers of Jesus who would be committed to work in the inner city in ministries that would help set the oppressed free, people of compassion who would be equipped to do lay counseling and develop support-group ministries. A picture of pastors and lay people coming to this place from other churches was forming in my spirit. They would come here to see what God was doing and take what they learned back to other churches throughout our denomination and beyond, promoting renewal.

Standing knee high in grass I envisioned a ministry that would focus equally on a personal relationship with Christ and social action. God is not only a God who hurts for the lost, but he also calls his people to be actively and aggressively involved in setting the oppressed free. (A reporter for the Dayton *Daily News* recently described Ginghamsburg church as a church that "combines conservative evangelical theology with strong social activism.")

When I left the field it was late afternoon. I left with a sunburn and a clear sense of God's purpose that has kept me moving forward and sustained me during my ministry at Ginghamsburg church. This experience has been the basis for everything else that has happened. The power of vision enabled me to see the reality of God's success before it happened.

When a leader has a clear picture of God's destination, the people begin to articulate and live that vision. Over a period of time that vision begins to penetrate the surrounding culture and even the secular newspaper can identify and articulate the missions objective.

Vision clarifies God's purpose and direction. When you clearly see God's purpose the obstacles that come will pale in comparison.

Doing Things "By the Book"

While the leader focuses on the end result, the manager tends to focus on the method or process. The manager wants to do things right according to organizational expectations—to go "by the book."

In my denomination's structure we have our yearly fall ritual of the nominating report. This form contains the many standardized offices and committees of the church. The manager rarely asks whether or not the labyrinth of committees is really needed to accomplish the mission of that particular church. They see it as their responsibility to "manage" the organizational structure. Many of our people end up wearing several different hats in the church as we attempt to fill in all of the slots. We challenge our people to become part of the greatest mission in the universe and then place them on a committee where they may do nothing more than argue over what kind of carpeting to put in the narthex.

I was recently invited to speak at a revival in a large church. The chairperson of the evangelism committee picked me up at the airport. I asked her what her committee had accomplished during the previous twelve months. She told me that my coming to their church was the result of their labors. Twelve people met ten times for the sake of having me come? One person could have picked up the phone and called me. It would have involved a simple five-minute telephone conversation. Look at how many valuable people hours were wasted.

Seventy percent of all baby-boomer women work today. Many of them are single parents. By the time they pick up their children at day care and get supper they have very little time left to invest in a committee that accomplishes next to nothing. We must be very selective in choosing the places that we ask people to spend their lives.

We have not had an evangelism committee in the 13 years that I have been at Ginghamsburg church. Evangelism is like breathing. It is the natural result of a healthy body. Your physical body doesn't need to have a breathing committee asking the question, "How are we going to breathe today?"

It is my goal to keep as few as possible in meetings and place the majority of key leaders in the direct front line mission of reaching the lost and setting the oppressed free. I have found that many people who come home from work exhausted and are consequently reluctant to give their time to committees are willing to work in front line mission that makes a difference in the lives of other people. They are willing to become involved in lay counseling programs, tutoring programs with children, support group and outreach ministries. These young working mothers and fathers are willing to give up Thanksgiving vacations to help rebuild homes for hurricane victims or serve dinner to the poor and lonely. They are willing to visit prisons and nursing homes, and to serve God's purpose through a resale clothing store, food pantry or furniture warehouse. People will give their time to answer telephones for crisis intervention ministries.

We have been too busy to have an evangelism committee, or, for that matter, to fill many of the slots on the nominating form. Maybe someday we will have the time to get around to it, but then evangelism will probably stop. We must move people from meetings to mission.

Jesus did not ask us to join a committee. He chose us that we might go out and "bear fruit in his name." The structure of the church exists for this purpose. It is only a vehicle to accomplish the mission of Christ.

We have a tendency in the church to make our structures an end in themselves. They become sacred calves that we begin to worship and serve. Structures should never be seen as sacred institutions that can never be adapted or even totally changed. They are temporary wineskins. Wineskins become brittle and need to be changed to hold next year's wine.

One structure that we tried to hold on to at Ginghamsburg church was the United Methodist Women. We tried for four years to make it work, but the young women we were attracting to our church did not relate to this wineskin. We had willingly changed all of our other traditional structures and it was working, but we had been unwilling to let go of this one ministry. United Methodist Women had become a golden calf for us.

My wife, Carolyn, got a group of women together and asked them what kinds of ministry would appeal to them and best meet their needs. They began aerobics programs, craft classes, Bible studies, evening programs for working women, a resale clothing store, and annual retreats with national speakers. These ministries attract many unchurched women from the surrounding communities and function from four to five days each week. The new wineskin is simply called "Women's Ministry." United Methodist Women has been a very key strategy for mission in the past. But it must never become a golden calf. The leader sees the goal and is willing to change structures for the purpose of reaching that goal. Accomplishing the mission of Christ is our goal, not serving the organizational structure. The structure must serve the goal.

The leader measures success by accomplishing right results, not by following the process of the structure.

The Leader Articulates the Vision

When I first came to Ginghamsburg church it was nown as the chicken noodle church. When I was ntroduced to several of the people in the community, was met with the response, "Oh, you are the chicken noodle pastor." For as long as anyone could remember, the church had focused its primary energies on two yearly chicken noodle dinners.

The older women of the church would pass the tradition down to the younger women by telling them the sacred traditions of the chicken noodle. They would relate how in days gone by the godmothers of the church would meet at the farmhouse next to the church and ring the chickens' necks and pluck feathers. People would work for a month to get ready for the sacred feast. Noodles were rolled and cut and then placed on long tables in the basement of the church for drying and seasoning.

Then the day of the sacred feast would finally arrive and people from all over Miami county would drive to the little country church to participate in the renowned Ginghamsburg chicken noodle dinner. Several hundred people would come. Every nook and cranny of this little church building was turned into a restaurant. People were served some of the best chicken noodles and homemade pies that you have ever tasted. When it was over people relaxed, feeling a deep sense of accomplishment, only later to remobilize for the next feast.[4]

Is this what God had in mind when he chose the church to be his hands and feet in the world? The Son of God gave his life for dinners and bazaars? The Bible clearly states that "without a vision the people perish." People need a challenging dream and clearly defined purpose.

The leader is one who is able to cast the dream. The leader must be able to answer the question about

why we are here. The business of Christ is not chicken
noodle dinners and bazaars. The business of Christ is
about winning the lost and setting the oppressed free.

Clearly articulated visions are compelling. They
attract people like magnets. Look at Dr. Kings' "I have
a dream." I can still see him delivering that message
from the steps of the Lincoln Memorial. His vision
still lives within me even though I was a young boy at
the time.

Mike Nygren, our youth director at Ginghamsburg church, is a dreamer. Incredible ministries have
been birthed through people who catch on fire with
his dreams. Four Clubhouse ministries operate
throughout the Dayton area. They are store-front
ministries (missions) that work with children. The
ministry includes tutoring in math and reading skills,
field trips, kid's clubs, gymnastics, summertime recreation programs, and an annual camp. Middle-class
teens from our church travel in vans after school into
areas infested with crack dealers to minister with
children. Adults leave work early to work alongside
the teens. As teens leave Mike's program for college
they take the vision with them. This year Clubhouses
were opened in Cincinnati and Oxford, Ohio, with
others being planned for Illinois and Indiana.

DreamBuilders is another of Mike's visions that
draws teens and adults together for the purpose of
building affordable, quality three-bedroom homes for
financially stressed families. The team members
begin framing the houses in the church parking lot
and then truck them to their final destination for
completion. Mike's team has already built three
homes in the Appalachian area of southeastern Ken-
tucky.

Over 500 houses in the Dayton area have been
insulated in cooperation with the Dayton Power and
Light Company through Mike's original concept of
the Dayton Work Project. President Bush personally

presented Mike and Monica Stratman (a teen worker)
with the 838th Point of Light Award for these ministries. It is not hard to see why Mike has no trouble
staffing his youth program with more than 50 adult
counselors. Visions are compelling. People need a
challenging vision and clearly articulated purpose.
They need to know that their lives and investments
of time are making a real difference.

Tom Sager, our pastor of care and counseling, has
been driven forward by God's dream of equipping
laity to do basic counseling. Over 100 Stephen ministers have been trained through Tom's ministry for the
ministry of caregiving. He also understood the need
for professional counseling at affordable prices. How
many people can afford counseling at $85 to $125 an
hour? The people of Ginghamsburg church were
caught up in Tom's vision and opened New Creation
Care Center this year. The center offers various support groups that deal with needs like eating disorders,
chemical addictions, sexual abuse and co-dependency.
Three professional counselors offer services from a
Christian perspective on a donation basis.

This is the business of Christ's church! Winning
the lost and setting the oppressed free! The leader is
able effectively to communicate that business. A
clearly articulated vision motivates and energizes
people. The leader understands that the people need
energy, vision and direction more than program
management. As Elisha said to Elijah, "I want a double
portion of the Spirit that is in you."

The Leader Clarifies the Mission:
Why are We Here?

If I went into the corporate offices of Coca Cola
Bottling Company in Atlanta, Georgia, and asked
anyone from the janitor to the CEO what the company's mission was they would be able to give me a

very clear, succinct answer—to sell Coca Cola. They
have been very effective in accomplishing their mission. Everywhere that I have traveled throughout the
world, from the most populated cities to remote
villages without electricity, I have found Coca Cola. I
was preaching in a rural village in India on the day
electricity first reached that area in 1975. They had
yet to experience electricity but they knew well the
taste of Coke.

When I ask the leaders of our churches the same
question—"What is your mission?"—their answer does
not have the same clarity of purpose. If the church
were as diligent as the Coca Cola Bottling Company,
this world would be evangelized.

The leader, through clear articulation of the
vision, is able to help the church define the mission.
The mission identifies the targets at which we are to
be aiming. If you aim at nothing you will surely hit
nothing. The mission enables the church to define the
allocation and forms of resources. We are not here for
chicken noodle dinners and bazaars. We are here to be
about Christ's purpose of reaching the lost and setting
the oppressed free. This means a radical realignment
of our focus, time, energy and resources.

My first goal in my ministry at Ginghamsburg
church was vision casting. I articulated Christ's vision
for the church from the pulpit, in meetings and with
those people whose hearts were "strangely warmed"
as they listened to the message. These people would
become key in my strategy to renew the church. I
began meeting with them in my home on Wednesday
evenings for the purpose of discipleship and with the
intent that they would move into key leadership
positions through the nominations process. This
"sanctified Amway" approach of involving people
who would in turn invest themselves and involve
others would become the basic strategy of ministry at
Ginghamsburg church. The strategy would involve a
process of multiplication. I would invest and repro-

duce myself in a small group of people who would
each invest and reproduce themselves. This was Jesus'
method of discipleship.

The second goal was to develop a clear mission
statement. A mission statement reminds us of our
purpose. It gives us permission not to do unnecessary
things and the focus to accomplish the essential. Jesus
was clear in his mission. "I was sent only to the lost
sheep of Israel" (Matthew 15:24, NIV). Peter would
later receive the vision that would open the gospel to
the gentile world.

The leadership went on a two-day retreat in my
eighth month of ministry at Ginghamsburg church
for the purpose of developing a mission statement.
This happened after eight months of vision casting.
Everyone had read George Hunter's book, *Contagious
Congregation,* before we went. We developed a mission statement that has gone through several revisions
since 1979. In its informal form, our mission statement
is "winning the lost and setting the oppressed free."
This is the business of Jesus and the focus of our energies and resources. If a meeting does not have as its
result winning the lost or setting the oppressed free,
why have it? We don't meet for the purpose of meeting. We meet for the purpose of accomplishing the
mission. Every person throughout the "organization"
needs to understand the mission. For Coca Cola it is
"sell Coke." For Ginghamsburg church it is "win the
lost and set the oppressed free."

The mission statement will take on a more formal form for the leadership—those involved in the
planning and direction of mission (see Figure 1). This
formal statement reminds us that success will not be
measured by numbers but by lives transformed
through the power of the Holy Spirit. People grow
into mature disciples through the balance of worship,
teaching, community and service. Christ is made
known through the process of equipping people to
reproduce this process in the lives of others.

Mission Statement
Ginghamsburg Church

Empowering people to know Jesus Christ as Lord through the transforming power of the Holy Spirit.

Experiencing growth in discipleship through worship, teaching, community and service.

Equipping people to make Christ known through the reproduction of this process in the lives of others.

Figure 1

What are We Going to Do?

The mission statement answers the question "why are we here?" The goal becomes even more specific in answering the question "what are we going to do?"

Our primary goal at Ginghamsburg church is found in Ephesians 4: 11-16.

> The gifts he gave were that some would be apostles, some prophets, some evangelists, some pastors and teachers, to equip the saints for the work of ministry, for building up the body of Christ, until all of us come to the unity of the faith and of the knowledge of the Son of God, to maturity, to the measure of the full stature of Christ (Ephesians 4:11-13).

Notice how pastoring is not the most important function in the church but only one among equals? The function of the pastor is not to do the ministry but for the purpose of preparing God's people for the work of ministry. I have not made more than 20-30 pastoral calls a year at Ginghamsburg church. It is not

my responsibility to make the calls. It is my responsibility to challenge and equip God's people to make
the calls.

The body of Christ is not an organization where a
few paid professionals can carry out the necessary
task. It is a living organism in which each part must
function according to its created purpose.

> ... into Christ, from whom the whole body,
> joined and knit together by every ligament
> with which it is equipped, as each part is
> working properly, promotes the body's
> growth in building itself up in love" (Ephe-
> sians 4: 15-16).

For the body to be healthy, every member must do its
part! This is our goal, to equip every person for the
purpose of becoming a fully assimilated, functioning
member of Christ's body (see Figure 2 on the next
page). We are not to be volunteers, but servants. Not
club members, but disciples, disciples who are able to
reproduce themselves in others.

How are We Going To Do It?

The leader is able to dream God's dreams, clearly
articulate the vision to the people, formulate goals
and ultimately turn the dream into reality through
the development and implementation of a strategy.
The strategy answers the question "how?"

After developing a mission statement and identi-
fying the goal of assimilation, we developed and
implemented the strategy of "assimilation circles"
(see Figure 3 on page 160). It is our goal to move each
person from outside the "target" through each of the
circles to the center.

Our first point of contact for many people would
be the worship celebration. Our worship experience
is put together with the needs of the unchurched in

An Assimilated Member

1. Has accepted Jesus Christ as Savior and Lord and shows evidence of a transformed lifestyle. (Values clarification)

2. Is publicly identified as a follower of Jesus. (By those outside of church)

3. Regularly participates in the celebration of corporate worship.

4. Has bought into the vision and mission of the church as evidenced through the personal sacrifice of time, talents and resources.

5. Practices a private devotional life through prayer, meditation and reflection on Scripture.

6. Has established important relationships within the body.

7. Is functioning in a significant responsibility as it relates to Christ's mission.

Figure 2

mind. Music, drama, prayer and message are always developed in light of outreach. We should not assume that the unchurched understand anything about the church and our traditions. Several years ago I was preaching a sermon about the Christmas story during Advent when a woman raised her hand and asked, "Who is Mary?" We live in a post-Christian age. Many American people have had minimal contact with the church and no exposure to the Bible.

An Assimilated Member

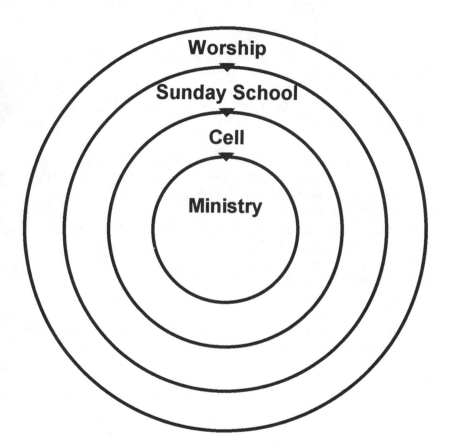

Figure 3

Our worship experience should make the unchurched feel like they were expected and their
questions anticipated. It should speak to their inner
hunger to know the God who created them for a
specific purpose. They should leave knowing that
God desires to be in a relationship with them and
they can know him in a personal way through Jesus
Christ. Warmth, practicality, excellence and pace are
all considerations in relating worship to the needs of
the unchurched.

Our next goal is to get the person involved in
Sunday school. This might be a class offered at a time
other than Sunday morning. Remember, we need to
find new wineskins to hold new wine. Many of our
classes are held at various times and days throughout
the week. Through the "Sunday school" experience
the person has an opportunity to begin developing
significant relationships and to begin to grow in
deeper ways through teaching and interaction. The
selection and training of teachers becomes critical to
the process at this point. We have a natural "hook" to
involve people at this level of growth. Our membership class, Vital Christianity, is a three-month class
offered on Sunday mornings and Wednesday evenings. By the way, it takes approximately three
months to form a habit!

The third level of growth is the cell or small-
group experience. It is at this level that real fellowship, or what the Bible calls *koinonia,* takes place. The
cell is the place of accountability and encouragement.
I can fake you out and appear spiritual in the larger
group, but when you really get to know me and your
wife talks to my wife every week on the phone, you
tend to discover my wrinkles and warts. It is in this
environment of unconditional love and challenge
that I discover the freedom to be real and open myself to the healing process of the Holy Spirit. True
depth in discipleship can happen only at this level.
Look at Jesus and his relationship with the twelve.

From the cell the people are encouraged to identify their "burning bush" and to begin to use their gifts and talents in ministry. The cell group's purpose is both to encourage by throwing gasoline on burning bushes, and to hold accountable by asking hard questions.

As they move through this process of assimilation their faith moves through stages, beginning with curiosity, growing to understanding, and then demonstrating itself in lifestyle commitment (see Figure 4 on the next page). The ultimate goal is for the disciple to be involved in reproducing this process in the lives of others.

The Leader Walks by Faith, Not Sight (The Work of the Spirit)

"This is the word of the LORD to Zerubbabel: Not by might, nor by power, but by my spirit, says the LORD of hosts. What are you, O great mountain? Before Zerubbabel you shall become a plain; and he shall bring out the top stone amid shouts of 'Grace, grace to it!'" (Zechariah 4:6-7)

Zerubbabel was chosen by God to be part of the restoration leadership team that would rebuild a demoralized covenant people upon their return from captivity in the fifth century, B.C. Jerusalem, the center and symbol of God's covenant and presence with his people, had been destroyed some 40-plus years before. God's people had literally become slaves in a foreign land.

Three men would assume very strategic roles of leadership in this restoration movement. Nehemiah, a wine steward for King Artaxerxes, was inspired by a vision to return to Israel to organize a movement that would result in rebuilding the walls around the once

The Process of Assimilation

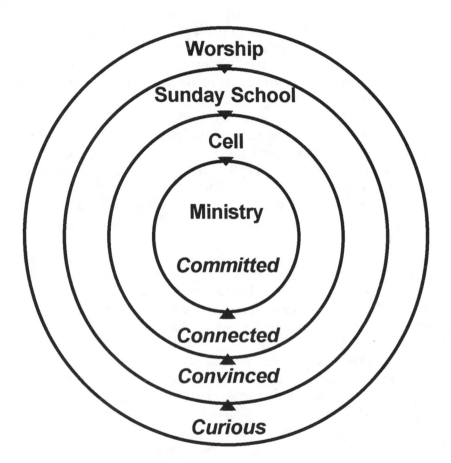

Figure 4

great city. Walls would provide defense against Israel's enemies. This strategic move would make a clear statement that God's people intended to be about God's business again. Ezra would function as the rebuilding priest. He would preside over the rebuilding of the spiritual life of God's people through the restoration of the temple and daily offerings. Zerubbabel was the contractor who would oversee the actual construction of the temple and the rebuilding of the altar.

From the very beginning these leaders met with resistance from every direction. The people had become greatly demoralized during their years of inactivity through captivity. They feared stepping out and risking great things in God's name. The pagan kings who lived in the area around Jerusalem were constantly making threats against their progressive intentions.

In the face of such resistance and opposition how would the work ever be accomplished? Zerubbabel had heard God's voice. "Not by might, nor by power, but by my spirit." God will go before us. God will overcome our obstacles. God will accomplish the seemingly impossible.

Renewal is God-breathed, not program planned. The institution tends to come up with a "program" that will promote change and growth. The leader realizes that ministry is Spirit-driven, not program-driven. The effective leader seeks to be more "charismatic" than "programmatic." Such leaders are able to stay focused on the unseen reality.

The king of Aram was at war with Israel. There was a leak in his military intelligence. Somehow Israel's king always got wind of his military strategies. The source turned out to be a prophet in Israel by the name of Elisha. Upon receiving this information, the king of Aram sent a major armored division to the city of Dothan to capture Elisha. They surrounded the city during the night. The next morning Elisha's servant was the first to notice the formidable obstacle. "What on earth are we going to do?" the worried servant asked. "How are we ever going to get out of this mess that your aggressive ministry style has gotten us into?"

Elisha was a leader who was focused on the unseen reality. Notice his response to the servant: "Do not be afraid, for there are more with us than there are with them" (2 Kings 6:16). The servant must think: "This guy is crazy! He must have had too much wine to drink last night." Now Elisha prays:

> "O LORD, please open his eyes that he may see." So the LORD opened the eyes of the servant, and he saw; the mountain was full of horses and chariots of fire all around Elisha (2 Kings 6:17).

Elisha is able to see the unseen. He doesn't become paralyzed by immediate pressures and obstacles. We are the people of the empty tomb. Empty tombs do not make sense. They are irrational. Empty tombs can occur only through the miraculous.

What do you do when your back is up against the Red Sea? Most of us in the church today would recommend forming a committee. After several months the committee comes back with a recommendation to build a bridge. Now we have to name a building committee. The building committee needs to secure the services of an architect. The architect comes back to the committee with several different designs. The committee needs to select a design and make a recommendation to the larger group. Now we have to have a building fund—which means another committee. We don't have time! When your back is up against the Red Sea and Pharaoh's army is breathing down your neck, wasting time means certain death. The solution can come only through the miraculous!

Look at the process most of us go through in establishing our church budgets. We set the budget by the amount of money that we think we can raise. If our pledge totals do not meet our budget proposals we often cut the budget back. This is walking by sight, not faith. We are planning ministry on the basis of our own limited supplies and resources rather than the unlimited supply of the God who parts the Red Sea and multiplies the loaves and fishes.

We do not announce our pledge totals at Ginghamsburg church made toward our annual budget. If we did that we might be tempted to set our budget by what we think we can do rather than the ministry God has called us to do. If God has called us to ministry then it is our responsibility to support that ministry regardless of the cost. God will supply the means. The ministry that he calls us to is a supernatural ministry. It can be accomplished only by the miraculous, not by what we can conceive, fund or pull off. That is why our income at Ginghamsburg church has grown from $27,000 to over $1,500,000 in 13 years. We believe that God is the God of the empty tomb!

The leader understands that the only limits to ministry are disobedience and limited vision. Effective leadership enables the church to stay focused on the unseen reality—to be the people of the empty tomb.

A good friend of mine led his small congregation through a period of growth and renewal that plateaued at an average worship attendance around 700. He told me that the people just decided to quit growing. It was never verbally stated. They were just not willing to take the same risks. They began to do ministry by what seemed "rationally possible." God will never support that which we attempt to do through our own strength, ability and resources. "Not by might, nor by power, but by my Spirit," says the Lord Almighty.

The Leader Functions
from Call and Giftedness

Leaders understand that they are called and set apart by God for a specific purpose. "Paul, called to be an apostle of Christ Jesus by the will of God. . ." (1 Corinthians 1:1). Paul knew that God had appointed him to be an apostle and that he would be held accountable by God for the ministry that he had been given. He was called to accomplish God's purpose. He was not sent to meet the expectations of the people.

This ministry flows from a Spirit dynamic. As the body of Jesus we can function in his purpose only through the Spirit of Jesus.

> The gifts he gave were that some would be apostles, some prophets, some evangelists, some pastors and teachers, to equip the saints for the work of ministry, for building up the body of Christ. . . . (Ephesians 4:11-12).

These "gifts of grace" are tools given by God for the purpose of accomplishing his purpose in the world. They are supernatural gifts, not human abilities. (See 1 Corinthians 12:1-11.)

Leaders understand God's specific call as well as their own particular gift mix. This enables the leader to focus on God's mission and not the institutional agenda.

At my first meeting with the Pastor-Parish Relations Committee I listed 12 pastoral functions on white meat-wrapping paper. You must understand we were a very small church and didn't have any chalk or marker boards. The 12 functions were pretty basic: preaching, home and hospital visitation, administration, teaching, youth, community involvement, counseling, ministry to shut-ins, fund raising, leadership, office functions (bulletin, newsletter, etc.), and worship. I asked each of the nine members to prioritize their expectations for my pastoral ministry from one to twelve on their own papers without looking at each other's lists.

After they were finished I asked them to share their lists of priorities with the whole group. Most of them were close in their first few priorities but they also saw that they had different expectations among themselves. I took a marker and circled my three areas of giftedness. I am a leader, a teacher, a motivator. This is what God has called me to be and has given me the gifts to do. My life is too short to be about anything else. If this doesn't fit with God's calling for mission in this place, ask me to leave and we can all be about that which is most important.

I have been very focused in my ministry at Ginghamsburg church. I have functioned from a clear sense of God's direction and call for my ministry. I spend my energy on the things that I know God has given me the gifts to do effectively and with which to produce results. I no longer spend my time on boards and committees that don't relate to my call and giftedness in the area of promoting renewal throughout the church. I do accept invitations to speak and do workshops throughout our denomination. I also periodically teach a class at a local seminary. These ministries mesh with God's call for my life. My energies in these areas produce fruit that coincides with God's gifts.

When I function in areas that are not related to my call or giftedness I find that I become frustrated, spiritually drained and ineffective. I do not have gifts in the area of pastoral care. Active listening is a skill that I still struggle to master. The details of day-to-day administration drive me nuts! I delegate these areas to others who are gifted with these skills. The right thing done by the wrong person is still wrong.

Each of us has been given just enough time to accomplish what God has called us and given us the gifts to do. Jesus, at the approximate age of 33, was able to say, "I have finished the work that you have given me." Jesus was focused on doing God's will through God's gifts. He did not surrender the precious commodity of time to accommodate the whims of people's expectations.

The Leader Inspires and Delegates: The Jethro Principle

Moses was just plain worn out. He was experiencing success. His leadership had resulted in a mass following, but the demands of the congregation had become overwhelming. There were not enough hours in the day to meet the growing needs of his people.

Jethro was Moses' father-in-law and a well-to-do theologian from Midian. During a family visit he noticed Moses' situation and posed a very strategic question (see Exodus 18): "Why are you trying to do this by yourself? What you are doing is not healthful. It is not good for you or the people you are doing it for." Actually much of what we do for people in the name of ministry supports co-dependent behavior in their lives as well as our own.

"You cannot go on this way forever, Moses," observed Jethro. "You will burn out and the people will never grow up. And more importantly, when do you ever have time for prayer? You need to be talking to God about these people. You are so busy dealing with their needs and expectations that you miss the opportunity to plug into the real power source."

Jethro then suggests a practical strategy for healthful, effective ministry. He tells Moses to:

1. *Pray* (verse 19). Focus on the unseen reality. It is God who goes before us. It is God who overcomes our obstacles. Only God can truly transform human lives.

2. *Teach* (verse 20). Moses must cast God's vision for the purpose of inspiring the people to obedient

action. The apostle Paul pointed out that people cannot believe if they don't hear the good news. And they cannot hear if there is no one to teach them. The ability to move people through teaching is indispensable to leadership. The goal of teaching is not information but transformation.

3. **Select capable people of integrity** (verse 21). People will follow people who model truth rather than just talk about it. We live in a time of much skepticism about the church. The church often seems to reflect the values and moral standards of the prevailing culture rather than the kingdom of God. People are hungry for an authentic alternative to the materialistic "me-ism" of our time. We need to identify those counter-culture individuals who are willing to demonstrate God's alternative community.

4. **Delegate** (verse 21-22). Give the ministry away. Just think of the number of people who can be ministered to if everything does not depend upon you! I can spend my time ministering to individual's needs or I can spend the same time equipping people to minister to others' needs. Which will bring the greatest results? If I minister to five people, five people will be ministered to. If I equip five people to do ministry and then each of us goes out and ministers to five more, we will be ministering to 30 people. It is a process of multiplication that can continue on indefinitely. My responsibility is to continue to work with my five for the purpose of vision, accountability and skill training.

Jethro outlines for Moses a clear line of accountability for ministry responsibility. The leaders of ten, cell pastors, will be the frontline delivery system for care and service. They will be the primary "pastor" for the people in their cell. If one of their people gets sick and goes to the hospital, they will be the pastor responsible for visitation. If there is a crisis in a member's family and children need to be cared for or food brought in, the leader of ten will take care of all the necessary arrangements. When a need arises that is beyond the cell pastor's expertise, she will contact her team pastor or leader of 50. The team pastor might determine a need for the depth of professional counseling and contact the coordinating pastor who is a leader of hundreds. At Ginghamsburg church our coordinating pastors are full-time staff. They are there for the purpose of selecting and equipping the leaders of 50 who select and equip the leaders of ten.

Carl George from Fuller Institute of Church Growth calls this the Meta Model of Ministry. This model provides for health and unlimited growth through the inspiration and delegation of ministry.

We call this ministry of inspiration and delegation the "Covenant Network" (see Figure 5 on the next page). As the pastor of leadership I spend three hours each week with the coordinating pastors. This time is used for Vision casting, Huddling for accountability and encouragement, and Skill training. This VHS model was inspired by Carl George. Each of the coordinating pastors meets with his or her team pastors in a Team meeting for the same purpose. The Team pastors meet with the cell pastors.

Many of our attempts at delegation fail because we do not follow up with a clear articulation of the vision, meet for the purpose of accountability, or give our people the necessary skills to carry out their responsibilities.

In Exodus 17 we read about Israel's battle against Amalek. Joshua led the army in battle while Moses observed the effort from the ridge of a distant hill. Moses understood this strategic purpose of vision casting as it related to Israel's success. As long as he held the staff of God up over his head where it could

The Covenant Network

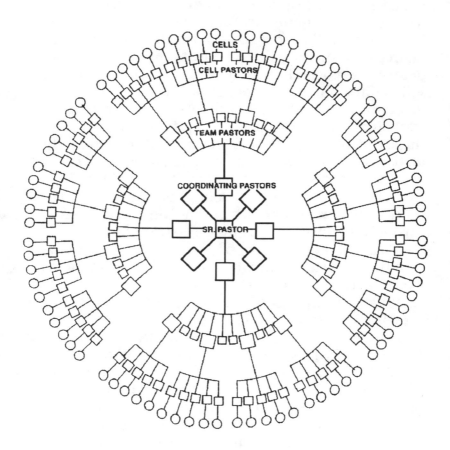

Figure 5

be seen by all, Israel prevailed. The staff represented the vision of God. It reminded the people of the God who goes before and delivers his people from the grip of oppression—the vision of God that parts the sea or brings water from a rock to quench thirst in the wilderness.

When Moses would get tired and lower the staff where it couldn't be seen, Israel would begin to lose. When the vision is not continually held high, the people will be defeated. Joshua finally wised up and sent Aaron and Hur up the hill to prop up Moses' arms until the outcome of the battle was assured.

An ongoing strategy for Vision casting, Huddling for encouragement and accountability and Skill training is absolutely essential in assuring the success of delegation. We do this in a monthly Team meeting at Ginghamsburg church. The leaders come together for supper at 6:30. After we eat we spend 10-15 minutes in praise and worship. I then spend 15-20 minutes articulating the Vision to all of the leaders of the church. The coordinating pastors then meet with the Team pastors for Huddle and Skill training. We have found that we can't always accomplish both during the same night. So we focus on Huddle one month and Skill training the next. The Team pastors then repeat this process with the cell pastors.

Jesus used this model of a ministry of inspiration and delegation. In Luke 9 he sends out the twelve (delegation) for the purpose of sharing the kingdom of God and being about God's ministry of healing. Notice the vision casting and skill training that takes place in Jesus' instruction to the disciples. "On their return the apostles told Jesus all they had done" (Luke 9:10). Jesus had in place a system of accountability. In Luke 10, Jesus repeats this process with 70 persons.

Delegation is the model used by Jesus and the true application of the "Priesthood Principle." Delegating ministry not only assures the health of the leaders and their families, it truly enables others to experience the fulfillment that is found in being used by God to fulfill his mission.

Leadership is influence! Leaders have the knowledge to influence others through inspiration and delegation to be involved in the mission of Jesus.

Leaders commit their energies to inspiring and delegating rather than doing ministry tasks.

The Leader Pays the Price

There is a price that goes with leadership. The leader is not going to be on everybody's most liked list. Leadership means risk and change and many people will resist change. It is easier to maintain the status quo. The leader who comes to a church and begins talking about moving forward and using new wineskins is going to be perceived by many as a boat rocker.

It is important for you to hear about my struggles in leading Ginghamsburg church. In my first two years of ministry I lost one-third of the congregation. Thirty of the 90 people left because they didn't want to grow and change. People openly stated that "this is our little church by the side of the road and we want it to stay that way!" Even though the loss was not reflected in the attendance figures because of new growth, it was still painful.

Marge and Joe graciously volunteered to baby-sit our daughter, who was only seven months old when we moved to Ginghamsburg. "After all," Marge beamed with the wisdom of a grandmother, "our own children live so far away, it will give us the opportunity to be active grandparents again."

We were very thankful for the diligent care and the gifts of much-needed breaks away from ministry that this kind couple gave Carolyn and me to get out one night a week, so it hurt that much more when Marge shared with us one Saturday evening: "We have decided to look for another church. It is not really that we blame you, Mike, but we just can't deal with the change."

I could hardly believe what I was hearing from this woman who was standing before me, rocking back and forth in an attempt to comfort my squirming baby daughter. The pain! It hurt!

We must be willing to pay the price of losing some people if we want to move forward and be about the business of Jesus. In the gospel of John we read that many of Jesus' disciples withdrew and followed him no more because they felt his teachings were "too hard." Jesus was willing to lose people for the sake of being faithful to God's truth. We must not compromise truth for the sake of pleasing people. This is God's church, not a human club.

Last summer during a time of reflection and listening prayer, the Spirit spoke to me from Jeremiah.

> Stand in the gate of the LORD's house, and proclaim there this word, and say, Hear the word of the LORD, all you people of Judah, you that enter these gates to worship the LORD. . . . Amend your ways and your doings, and let me dwell with you (Jeremiah 7: 2-3).

Our church was struggling with the problem of immaturity. Many of us are bowing down to the golden calves of our culture and forsaking our first love. I knew that I had to deal with this issue openly and honestly if we were to continue to move forward and not bog down in the wilderness.

During the fall of 1992, our attendance dropped 150-200 over a two-month period after I began preaching a series on "growing up." This was a scary experience! In 20 years of ministry I had never been a part of something moving backward. If I had not so clearly heard God's voice that summer to call the people to a lifestyle of integrity, I would have been tempted to change the message. But I am committed to respond to the voice of God and not the will of people. Who knows what the cost may be? You can never really be sure—only faithful.

Our attendance began to rebound and grow again during the winter of 1992-93. We have recently purchased 100 acres of land on Interstate 75 and hope to begin construction on our new church facility before spring of 1994.

Leaders are willing to pay the price. They are fully invested. They have committed their resources and energy to the purpose for which God has called them. Great leaders are willing to die for the cause that they believe so strongly. When Dr. King was asked about the precarious nature of his future he responded by saying, "Sure, I would love to live a long life. Longevity is much to be desired. But I must accomplish the will of God for my life."

Most people have not found anything in life that is really gripping and fulfilling. You will never discover life until you find that which is worth dying for. The leader moves through life demonstrating the passion for that for which it is worth dying. People follow people who are being used up for something greater than personal gain. People will follow leaders who are truly going the way of the Cross.

The leader must be willing to pay the price. There is no shortcut to the hard work and sacrifice that goes with the ministry of discipleship.

Integrity

George Barna, founder of the Barna Research Group, tells us that church attendance is on the way down. He predicts that church attendance on Sunday morning will decrease from the current 42 percent of the population to 35 percent on any given Sunday morning by the year 2000.[5] Greater numbers of people are finding the institutional church to be irrelevant to their needs. Many of the baby boomers who began returning to the church in the mid 1980s are beginning to leave at an alarming rate, feeling that the

church is still as impotent as they remembered it to b
from their childhood.

People don't need more information. Our churches have mastered the art of giving informational
programs for successful living. We offer countless
seminars where people come and fill notebooks with
our simplistic formulas. People in the 1990s need to
see a demonstration of authentic kingdom living.
They need to experience caring relationships.

It is easier to preach the Word than walk the
Word. Many pastoral homes have suffered the conse-
quence of informational ministry that has left no
time for authentic kingdom living in the home. Our
people have become wise to these inconsistencies and
are beginning to look for answers outside the church.
Divorce among clergy is increasing at an alarming
rate.

Last year I received an invitation from Robert
Schuller to participate and dialogue with a group of
50 pastors in the formation of Churches Uniting in
Global Mission. We would spend two days together
and each of us was to come prepared to share with the
group "the most significant thing that I am doing in
ministry." I wrestled with this topic for a month.
"What am I going to say? What of significance do I
have to share with these pastors who come from
churches that are so much bigger than Ginghamsburg
church?"

When I arrived in Anaheim, California, I was still
uncertain about my report. We were to give our pre-
sentations in alphabetical order, so that bought me
some time. These pastors were from the largest
churches in America. Many of them had been my
heroes. They were doing incredible ministries as local
churches. One had just opened a church in Russia,
another a 250-bed hospital in Zaire. I had nothing new
to offer of any significance.

My turn came—what is the most significant thing
that I am doing in ministry? It hit me. "The most sig-

ficant ministry that I am having at this moment is coaching my son's baseball team." I said that and sat down. All the way to Anaheim, California, and back to declare that my most immediate, important ministry was working with my son? That's it! Demonstrating the priority and lifestyle of the kingdom of God. Letting people "see" the difference that Jesus makes.

Leadership in the 1990s and beyond will be committed to lifestyle integrity. The church must be a live demonstration on earth of what's going on in heaven. We must demonstrate God's values toward people. We must take responsibility for the stewardship of his planet as it relates to the environment and every living creature. We must demonstrate our love for God as we honor the covenants that we have made with our families. The world is looking for a living demonstration, not more information. Kingdom leaders are living examples of walking with—not talking about—God.

It is my prayer that these six principles will not be taken as a simplistic formula for the promotion of institutional growth. Church growth is not the goal. The goal is transformational renewal. True renewal is God-breathed, not program-planned.

God desires and wills renewal. He has committed the life of his Son for the purpose of reconciling and restoring the whole of the planet earth. You and I have been called to participate with God in this mission. He wills our success. The "signs and wonders" of God's presence and transforming power are not intended only for a handful of churches like Ginghamsburg church. God is actively and aggressively seeking all who are willing to dream and risk his purpose. He is calling his people back to first principles—to their first love.

Dare to be the people of the empty tomb!

Notes

1 Warren Bennis and Burt Nanus, *Leaders: The Strategies for Taking Charge*. Harper and Row, Publishers, New York, 1985, 2.

2 The name "Counter-Reformation" seems inappropriate in the sense that the movement was renewing faith and focus in the Catholic Church, not countering what the Protestant reformers were doing.

3 Bennis and Nanus, 21.

4 There was one other yearly event—the annual Christmas Bazaar. People would spend from July to November making crafts for the purpose or raising money for mission. A bazaar is not the most efficient use of time or money to raise money for mission. It is much more effective just to take the money from our pockets to serve Christ's purpose.

5 George Barna, *The Frog in the Kettle*. Regal Books, Ventura, California, 1990, 142.

Appendix A

Vital Christianity

Course Outline

LIFE IN CHRIST

Week 1: Introduction and Expectations: Who Is Jesus?

Week 2: Who Is Jesus?

Week 3: What Is a Christian?

Week 4: The Lordship of Christ

LIFE IN THE SPIRIT

Week 5: Who Is the Holy Spirit?

Week 6: Fruit of the Spirit

Week 7: Gifts of the Spirit

Week 8: Spiritual Disciplines

LIFE IN COMMUNITY

Week 9: What Is the Church?

Week 10: What Is Ministry?

Week 11: How Do I Discover My Call?

Week 12: Commitment to Serve

Week 13: Sharing Your Spiritual Journey

Between weeks 4 and 5: Fellowship Event

Between weeks 8 and 9: Fellowship Event

After week 12 or 13:   Dinner with Pastor's Talk

Appendix B

Rules of the Band-Societies

Drawn up December 25, 1738

The design of our meeting is to obey that command of God, "Confess your faults one to another, and pray one for another, that ye may be healed."

To this end, we intend, —

1. To meet once a week, at the least.
2. To come punctually at the hour appointed, without some extraordinary reason.
3. To begin (those of us who are present) exactly at the hour, with singing or prayer.
4. To speak, each of us in order, freely and plainly, the true state of our souls, with the faults we have committed in thought, word, or deed, and the temptations we have felt since our last meeting.
5. To end every meeting with prayer, suited to the state of each person present.
6. To desire some person among us to speak *his* own state first, and then to ask the rest in order as many and as searching questions as may be concerning their state, sins, and temptations.

Some of the questions proposed to everyone before *he* is admitted among us may be to this effect:

1. Have you the forgiveness of your sins?
2. Have you peace with God, through our Lord Jesus Christ?
3. Have you the witness of God's Spirit with your spirit that you are a child of God?

4. Is the love of God shed abroad in your heart?

5. Has no sin, inward or outward, dominion over you?

6. Do you desire to be told of your faults?

7. Do you desire to be told of all your faults, and that plain and home?

8. Do you desire that every one of us should tell you, from time to time, whatsoever is in *his* heart concerning you?

9. Consider! Do you desire we should tell you whatsoever we think, whatsoever we fear, whatsoever we hear, concerning you?

10. Do you desire that in doing this we should come as close as possible, that we should cut to the quick, and search your heart to the bottom?

11. Is it your desire and design to be on this and all other occasions entirely open, so as to speak everything that is in your heart without exception, without disguise, and without reserve?

Any of the preceding questions may be asked as often as occasion offers; the [four] following at every meeting:

1. What known sins have you committed since our last meeting?

2. What temptations have you met with?

3. How [were] you delivered?

4. What have you thought, said, or done, of which you doubt whether it be sin or not?

Rupert E. Davis, ed., *The Works of John Wesley* (Nashville: Abingdon, 1989), vol. 9, *The Methodist Societies: History, Nature, and Design,* 77-78.

Directions Given to the Band Societies

December 25, 1744

You are supposed to have the "faith that over-cometh the world." To you therefore it is not grievous,

I. Carefully to abstain from doing evil; in particular,

    1. Neither to *buy nor sell* anything at all on the Lord's day.

    2. To taste no spirituous liquor, *no dram* of any kind, unless prescribed by a Physician.

    3. To be *at a word* both in buying and selling.

    4. To *pawn nothing,* no, not to save life.

    5. Not to *mention the fault* of any *behind his back,* and to stop those short that do.

    6. To wear no *needless ornaments,* such as rings, ear-rings, necklaces, lace, ruffles.

    7. To use no *needless self-indulgence,* such as taking snuff or tobacco, unless prescribed by a Physician.

II. Zealously to maintain good works; in particular,

    1. To *give alms* of such things as you possess, and that to the uttermost of your power.

    2. To *reprove* all that sin in your sight, and that in love and meekness of wisdom.

    3. To be patterns of *diligence* and *frugality,* of *self-denial,* and taking up the cross daily.

III.   Constantly to attend on all the ordinances of God; in particular,

  1.   To be at church, and at the Lord's table, every week, and at every public meeting of the bands.

  2.   To attend the ministry of the Word every morning, unless distance, business, or sickness prevent.

  3.   To use private prayer every day, and family prayer if you are at the head of a family.

  4.   To read the Scriptures, and meditate thereon, at every vacant hour. And,

  5.   To observe as days of fasting or abstinence all *Fridays* in the year.

Rupert E. Davis, ed., *The Works of John Wesley* (Nashville: Abingdon, 1989), vol. 9, *The Methodist Societies: History, Nature, and Design,* 79.

Appendix C

Teacher's Covenant

Ginghamsburg Church

Recognizing the high privilege that I have to serve the Lord Jesus through our Sunday school, and trusting in the guidance and empowerment of the Holy Spirit, I pledge myself to this covenant.

1. Because the Lord wants the best in me and through me:

   I am a member or am in the process of becoming a member of Ginghamsburg United Methodist Church.

   I will live what I teach concerning lifestyle and personal integrity. (1 Thessalonians 5:22)

   I will regularly attend and urge members of my class to attend worship services.

   I will be faithful in attendance at Sunday school. If, at any time, through sickness or other emergency, I am unable to teach my class, I will notify the education supervisor at the earliest possible time. (1 Corinthians 4:2)

2. Because the Lord wants the best for my class:

   I will show a deep spiritual concern for the members of my class. My desire will be to bring about the opportunity for each person to know Jesus Christ as personal Savior and Lord and to encourage the spiritual growth of each Christian.

I will provide for the shepherding needs of my class and follow-up on or provide follow-up for class members with needed care—absences, illness, family crises, etc.

I will carefully prepare my lessons and make each lesson a matter of earnest prayer.

3. Because the Lord wants the best for the church and its Sunday school ministry:

I will act on discipleship principles and, when possible, identify and nurture an apprentice to work with me and to eventually be released to teach.

I will give support to the Sunday school program by:

> attending at least four of the six bi-monthly teachers' meetings and training sessions.

> covering all administrative procedures and information gathering needed by the Sunday school (attendance, offering, etc.)

I will meet with the Adult Sunday School Coordinator periodically for dialog, input and mutual decision making regarding continuation of my class.

Signed _____

Date _____

Recognizing the responsibility given for educating, nurturing, and raising up mature disciples, the Adult Education Committee pledges the following to its teachers:

1. To provide high quality and motivational training to adult Sunday school teachers in order to equip and enable them to disciple adults at Ginghamsburg United Methodist Church.

2. To provide resources needed (space, materials etc.) to creatively and inspirationally teach adult Sunday school classes.

3. To support and encourage teachers relationally and to operate under a system of mutual accountability in order to build up and disciple each other.

4. To provide necessary administrative support.

5. To provide clear lines of communication in order to share the mission and vision of Ginghamsburg United Methodist Church with the teachers so they can do the same with their classes.

Signed_____
Adult Sunday School Coordinator

Date _____

Signed _____
Director of Education and Congregational Life

Date _____

Appendix D

Ministries that were Dreamed, Developed, and Staffed by the People of Ginghamsburg Church

The Clothesline

This is a clothing resale store located about one block from Ginghamsburg church. It is open 4 days per week, is staffed by volunteers and has been in operation for approximately 12 years. In addition to donating clothing and baskets to needy persons, the Clothesline also gives support to the Christmas families. The Clothesline disperses its profits monthly to causes that benefit individuals and groups in both the church and the surrounding community. In addition, a financial commitment has been made to support the Clubhouse ministries and also an Indian boy in Oklahoma.

The Clubhouse

Actually, this refers to Clubhouses! Beginning as an after-school reading program in a local housing project, the Clubhouse ministry has expanded into three locations currently in operation. Each Clubhouse is staffed by a teen intern and teen workers throughout the school year. We have two full-time staff persons at Ginghamsburg church dedicated to the Clubhouse children and to nurturing and discipling the teens who lead the children. This year we operated a three-day summer camp for the Clubhouse children for more teaching time and relationship building with the children. At present the Clubhouse ministry is extending beyond our local Clubhouses. As our teens graduate from high school and go on to college, five of them have taken the knowledge, training and skills learned at Ginghamsburg and have opened Clubhouses in other cities. Another high school graduate led a summer Clubhouse four-week session for children of migrant workers in our area. Plans are being made for Clubhouses in other locations.

Community Relief

This ministry provides material and financial assistance to non-members of Ginghamsburg church by helping with rent, utilities, medical expenses and other basic needs. It also acts as a referral system to inform people of various resources available to them.

DreamBuilders

Still in the planning stages, but definitely on its way, DreamBuilders intends to rehabilitate homes in the Dayton area and provide affordable housing for low income families who would otherwise be unable to own a home. This project would combine the learnings of various past building experiences, link teen and adult mission efforts within our own community, and provide construction experience and ministry to our teens and adults on a year-round basis. In addition, DreamBuilders will continue its ministry in Appalachia by constructing new homes in that part of the country.

Food Pantry

Our food pantry volunteer team distributes food as needed to persons within the church as well as the community. In addition to delivering the food, our volunteers listen to people's needs and hurts and share words of hope from the Bible. The youth group supports the food pantry with an annual food collection.

Furniture Warehouse

The furniture warehouse provides used furniture to those in need and enables the members of Ginghamsburg church to share their abundance with others. The warehouse accepts furniture from many sources, refurbishes it, and distributes it with love, and with no obligation, to those in need. Also, the warehouse volunteers regularly load a truck with excess clothing and furniture and deliver the items to distribution locations in Appalachia.

H.E.L.P.

The "Home Environment Labor Partners" concept allows our members to provide assistance for maintenance needs and daily tasks to those who are elderly, disabled, widowed or in financial stress. These tasks include minor home repair, auto maintenance, painting and other services.

Love Fund

Members of Ginghamsburg church can receive financial and material assistance as required in times of temporary crisis or unusual situations. This is a way in which we share what Jesus has given us with others in our body. All that is required is a need to be expressed. This fund is designed to furnish the means to overcome those difficult times with dignity.

New Creation Care Center

New Creation Care Center is a ministry that seeks to respond to persons in pain. Through our counselors, our Stephen Ministers, and our support groups, we offer distinctively Christian support and healing. Because we believe Jesus Christ is the ultimate answer to our needs, we want to help persons grow in their relationships with Christ, and in particular, to apply his healing presence and love at the point of their needs. We understand that this is neither a simple nor a magical procedure, but rather a gradual and profound process of moving further into spiritual and emotional wholeness through Christ.

The New Creation Care Center has its own facility, a recently renovated church building. At present more than 35 Stephen Ministers and four professional counselors lead the ministry endeavors. The center is under the direction of a full-time pastor who has responsibility for care and counseling at Ginghamsburg church.

Nursing Home Ministry

Our nursing home outreach seeks to connect persons in Ginghamsburg church with nursing home residents, offering companionship, love, care and sharing of God's Word in worship and song. We also provide large print Bibles and offer Bible study both individually and as group sharing. Our intent is to provide on-going relationship and caring.

Prison Ministry

Persons involved in the prison ministry witness to inmates through friendship, time, love and gifts. We seek to lift up people in despair and loneliness by providing them with the Lord's Word and the actions of caring Christians. A central part of the ministry is the pen pal program which links the inmates with someone outside the prison.

Women's Center

This is a Christian pro-life outreach to the community and an abortion-alternative center. This ministry provides counseling, support and the sharing of the Word while maintaining the client's anonymity. Pregnancy testing is also offered at no charge or obligation. The center is self-supporting.

Preschool Ministry

Currently 95 children participate in our five-day a week preschool program. About 80 percent of these 3- to 5-year-old children come from unchurched families.

Principles of Church Renewal
Bibliography

ANDERSON, James D. and JONES, Ezra Earl.
1986   *Ministry of the Laity.* San Francisco, Harper and Row Publishers.

ANDERSON, Leith.
1990   *Dying for Change.* Minneapolis, Minnesota, Bethany House Publishers.

ARN, Win and ARN, Charles.
1982   *The Master's Plan for Making Disciples.* Pasadena, California, Church Growth Press.

BAINTON, Roland.
1950   *Here I Stand: A Life of Martin Luther.* Nashville: Abingdon.

BARNA, George.
1992   *The Barna Report 1992-93.* Ventura, California: Regal Books.
1992   *Church Marketing.* Ventura, California: Regal Books.
1990   *The Frog in the Kettle.* Ventura, California: Regal Books.
1992   *The Power of Vision.* Ventura, California: Regal Books.
1991   *User Friendly Churches.* Ventura, California: Regal Books.

BONHOEFFER, Dietrich.
1949   *The Cost of Discipleship.* New York: MacMillan Publishing Co., Inc.

BURTNER, Robert W. and CHILES, Robert E.
   1954   *A Compend of Wesley's Theology.* Nashville:
          Abingdon.

CALLAHAN, Kennon L.
   1983   *Twelve Keys to an Effective Church: Strategic
          Planning for Mission.* San Francisco: Harper and
          Row.

CHANEY, Charles L. and LEWIS, Ron S.
   1977   *Design for Church Growth.* Nashville: Broadman
          Press.

CHILES, Robert E.
   1984   *Scriptural Christianity: A Call to John Wesley's
          Disciples.* Grand Rapids, Michigan: Francis Asbury
          Press, Zondervan Corporation.

CHO, Paul Yonggi.
   1984   *More Than Numbers.* Word Books.

COLEMAN, Robert E.
   1963   *The Master Plan of Evangelism.* Old Tappan,
          New Jersey: Fleming H. Revell Company.

CURNOCK, Nehemiah, ed.
   1909   *The Journal of John Wesley, A.M.* New York: Eaton
          and Mains.

DESCHNER, John.
   1960   *Wesley's Christology.* Dallas: Southern Methodist
          University Press.

DICKENS, A. G.
   1969   *The Counter Reformation.* Great Britain: Har-
          court, Brace, and World.

EIMS, Leroy.
   1978   *The Lost Art of Disciple Making.* Grand Rapids,
          Michigan: Zondervan Publishing House.

ELLER, Vernard.
   1980   *The Outward Bound: Caravaning as the Style of
          the Church.* Grand Rapids, Michigan: William B.
          Eerdmans Publishing Company.

FOAKES-JACKSON, F. J.
   1927   *History of the Christian Church to A.D. 461.*
          Chicago. W. P. Blessing, Company.

GALLAWAY, Ira.
   1983   *Drifted Away: Returning the Church to Witness and Ministry.* Nashville: Abingdon.

GAUSTAD, Edwin Scott, ed.
   1974   *The Rise of Adventism.* New York: Harper and Row, Publishers.

GEORGE, Carl F.
   1991   *Prepare Your Church for the Future.* Grand Rapids, Michigan: Fleming H. Revell.

GREEN, Hollis L.
   1972   *Why Churches Die: A Basic Guide to Evangelism and Church Growth.* Minneapolis: Bethany Fellowship.

HUNTER, George G., III.
   1979   *The Contagious Congregation.* Nashville: Abingdon.
   1987   *To Spread the Power: Church Growth in the Wesleyan Spirit.* Nashville: Abingdon.

JOHNSON, Douglas W. and WALTZ, Alan K.
   1987   *Fact and Possibilities: An Agenda for The United Methodist Church.* Nashville: Abingdon.

KELLY, Dean M.
   1972   *Why Conservative Churches are Growing.* New York: Harper and Row.

KERR, Hugh T. and MULDER, John M., editors.
   1983   *Conversions: The Christian Experience.* Grand Rapids, Michigan: Eerdmans Publishing House.

MCGAVRAN, Donald A.
   1980   *Understanding Church Growth.* Revised ed., Grand Rapids, Michigan: Eerdmans Publishing House.

MCGAVRAN, Donald A. and ARN, Winfield C.
   1973   *How to Grow a Church.* Glendale, California: Regal Books.
   1977   *Ten Steps for Church Growth.* San Francisco: Harper and Row.
   1981   *Back to Basics in Church Growth.* Wheaton, Illinois: Tyndale House Publishers.

MCGAVRAN, Donald with HUNTER, George III, edited by
Lyle Schaller
  1980   *Church Growth: Strategies that Work.* Nashville:
          Abingdon.

MCLOUGHLIN, William G.
  1978   *Revivals, Awakenings, and Reform: An Essay on
          Religion and Social Change in America, 1607-
          1977.* Chicago: University of Chicago Press.

MILLER, Herb with SCHALLER, Lyle, editor.
  1987   *How to Build a Magnetic Church.* Nashville:
          Abingdon.

NICHOLS, James Hastings.
  1968   *Corporate Worship in the Reformed Tradition.*
          Philadelphia: The Westminster Press.

O'CONNOR, Elizabeth
  1963   *Call to Commitment.* New York: Harper and Row.
  1968   *Journey Inward, Journey Outward.* New York:
          Harper and Row.

PHIFER, Kenneth G.
  1965   *A Protestant Case for Liturgical Renewal.* Phila-
          delphia: The Westminster Press.

SCHALLER, Lyle E.
  1987   *It's A Different World.* Nashville, Abingdon.
  1985   *The Middle-Sized Church.* Nashville: Abingdon.
  1983   *Growing Plans: Strategies to Increase Your
          Church's Membership.* Nashville: Abingdon.

SNYDER, Howard A.
  1977   *The Community of the King.* Downer's Grove:
          InterVarsity Press.
  1976   *The Problem of Wineskins: Church Structure in a
          Technological Age.* Downer's Grove: InterVarsity
          Press.
  1980   *The Radical Wesley and Patterns for Church
          Renewal.* Downer's Grove: InterVarsity Press.

STEDMAN, Ray C.
  1972   *Body Life.* Glendale, California: Regal Books.

TILLAPAUGH, Frank R.
   1982   *The Church Unleashed: Getting God's People Out
           Where the Needs Are.* Ventura, California: Regal
           Books.

TRUEBLOOD, Elton.
   1980   *The Company of the Committed.* San Francisco:
           Harper and Row.

VAUGHAN, John N.
   1985   *The Large Church: A Twentieth-Century Expres-
           sion of the First-Century Church.* Grand Rapids,
           Michigan: Baker Book House.

WAGNER, C. Peter.
   1984   *Leading your Church to Growth.* Ventura, Califor-
           nia: Regal Books.
   1987   *Strategies for Church Growth.* Ventura, California:
           Regal Books.
   1976   *Your Church Can Grow: Seven Vital Signs of a
           Healthy Church.* Glendale, California: Regal
           Books.

WAGNER, C. Peter, editor with ARN, Win and TOWNS,
Elmer.
   1986   *Church Growth, State of the Art.* Wheaton, Illi-
           nois: Tyndale House Publishers.

WATSON, David Lowes.
   1987   *The Early Methodist Class Meeting: Its Origins
           and Significance.* Nashville: Discipleship Re-
           sources, Abingdon.

WESTERHOFF, John H., III.
   1985   *Living the Faith Community: The Church That
           Makes a Difference.* San Francisco: Harper and
           Row.

WILKE, Richard E.
   1986   *And Are We Yet Alive?* Nashville: Abingdon.

WILLIMON, William H. and WILSON, Robert L.
   1987   *Rekindling the Flame: Strategies for a Vital
           United Methodism.* Nashville: Abingdon.